'**Assessment must have a purpose**.
Assessment for its own sake has no intrinsic value.

What it looks like

This principle is evident when these criteria may be observed:

- Practitioners listen to and note children's reactions to and involvement in their learning and respond in ways which support that learning there and then.

- Assessment provides an insight into how best to help a child develop and learn. What practitioners look at, listen to and note is fully considered to plan the next steps in learning.

- The effect of provision on children's development and learning is examined carefully. Practitioners use this information to investigate whether what they are doing is having a positive impact.'

Creating the Picture (Department for Education and Skills, 2007)

CATCHING THEM AT IT!

Assessment in the early years

Sally Featherstone

Published 2011 by A&C Black Publishers Limited
36 Soho Square, London W1D 3QY
www.acblack.com

ISBN 978-1-4081-3115-2

Text © Sally Featherstone, 2011
Design by Bob Vickers

Printed in Great Britain by Latimer Trend & Company Limited

This book is produced using paper that is made from wood grown in
managed, sustainable forests. It is natural, renewable and recyclable.
The logging and manufacturing processes conform to the
environmental regulations of the country of origin.

To see our full range of titles
visit www.acblack.com

Contents

Preface: A brief history of assessment

In my long life in early years education, I have been fortunate to experience many developments, fashions, theories, methods and guidance on assessment of learning and attainment. In their time each was a professional, well-meaning attempt to find out and record what children were learning. Some of the initiatives were successful and helpful in the work of practitioners, some were certainly not; some were time consuming, some took almost no time; and of course, some were useful, some were not. My experience as a practitioner has been in England, but this short journey through previous methods will probably make sense across the globe, wherever young children are cared for and educated outside the home.

Previous assessment methods

This small selection is not in chronological order because some methods were fashionable simultaneously in different settings.

The Medical Milestones model

In the days when nursery provision was more about care and less about learning, sets of developmental milestones were devised (often in consultation with the medical profession) and published to help parents and childcare workers to check whether children were growing and developing normally. They were based on average growth and weight statistics, and they listed the things babies and young children were expected to do at different ages, from birth to around five, when children started school. Teachers and nursery nurses adopted and used these developmental checklists to assess children's progress in day nurseries and nursery schools.

Milestones checklists are still popular and readily available through the Internet. Many parents can access and use them to assess the progress of their babies and children. They have not been used in isolation in daycare since governments became interested in the educational advantages of early education, and incorporated the milestones into assessment schedules.

The problems

These checklists didn't have any leeway for individuals or for the range of normal growth across a group of children, and like all checklists, they were statements with yes/no answers. The simple nature of the assessment can lead to unnecessary concern about individual children, particularly by parents. The milestones focused almost entirely on physical and language development, giving a very narrow view of individual babies and children.

What this method looks like now

Of course all early years practitioners need to know about child development, and what is generally considered to be the normal path of development for babies and young children. The Early Years Foundation Stage (EYFS) Development Matters Statements in England have given a new look to 'milestones' statements by setting them out in overlapping stages to give a more gentle progression with more space for individual differences in development. They have also been broadened beyond easily observable features to include social, emotional, creative and other aspects of development and learning.

The 'Catch it if you see it, and wait for the 11+' model

This is where teachers collected random information about children when they saw it, often keeping this information in their heads until they completed annual reports or talked to parents and colleagues. At the time, there was no National Curriculum, so there was no written description of the desired outcomes of the education system. Teachers did the best they could in assessing children by chance in the early years.

Some nursery classes and schools constructed checklists of expectations, often based on the milestones model. Written records were not universal, and written reports to parents were rare for children in the early years. Children with additional needs were not usually referred, tested or diagnosed by a psychologist until they were seven years old.

The only national test was the 11+, a written test of English, mathematics and general knowledge, taken by all children at the end of primary school. About ten per cent of children passed the 11+ and went to grammar schools, the rest failed and went to secondary schools. The central purpose of this test was to identify the children most able to pass this sort of test who, it was therefore deemed would benefit from grammar school education.

The problems

Although this very informal method took very little time to implement, it was possible to get by without collecting any information at all about some individuals or some aspects of development. There was little written or formal curriculum planning, and the practical nature of the early years curriculum meant that there was no marking or grading. The information gathered about individual children remained in the heads of their teachers and was often affected by the random nature of all informal collection.

What this method looks like now

There are still some early years practitioners who think that the 'Catch it if you see it' model is the best one, and are reluctant to adopt a more systematic collection of assessment evidence through observation, particularly because it is more time consuming. However, the Qualifications and Curriculum Development Agency (QCDA) advice to practitioners in England very clearly states that: 'Ongoing assessment is an integral part of the learning and development process.' It emphasises the importance of systematic observation across all areas, and this is therefore integral to every practitioner's job.

The 'If it moves, write about it' model

In this model, teachers and other adults working in the early years wrote lengthy and lovingly crafted 'stories' about each child. These were descriptive accounts of the child and long observations of activities, which were filed in huge ring binders. These were seldom re-read or evaluated and rarely influenced what was planned next. The stories were written during the year and were sometimes summed up in an even longer discursive prose statement at the end of the year.

A few nurseries and schools made a short version of the stories for the next teacher, and in these cases the original work was discarded. In others, the whole huge volume was transferred and often it was never read. Only in the most exceptional settings did parents and the children themselves ever know about their own learning stories, and practitioners seldom used them for planning.

The problems

Records of this sort were extremely time consuming, seen as a real chore, and were such a waste of time, because the information collected was rarely used to change anything. The stories were given to the next teacher who often received several fat files of handwritten stories which they had no time or interest in reading, so they often ignored the files and just started where they always had done with a new class.

What this method looks like now

Of course, long observations of individual children are still a very valid way of finding out what they know and can do. But now practitioners realise that the observations are of little use unless adults respond to the information they have collected. We also know that the information handed on to the next practitioner or teacher must be both manageable *and* useful, and that huge volumes of unsorted information are usually disregarded.

The 'Let's knit one ourselves' model

This is where teachers and their assistants (usually nursery nurses), unable to find a model that exactly suited the needs of the children, constructed schedules for assessment themselves, calling these personal profiles or records. The schedules were carefully put together to help adults, and sometimes parents, to understand how well individual children were doing. Groups of teachers and other practitioners tried to systematically cover all aspects of children's learning, and these schedules were an attempt to make children's records more robust and systematic. Most were completed once a term, with a final judgement made near the end of the summer term to prepare for parents' evenings and transfer to the next class.

The problems

Because the need to plan for assessment had not been recognised, these records, although conscientiously constructed, were often completed without the child present. The judgements made by adults were, therefore, based on what they could remember of a child. This sometimes lead to errors and a bit of guesswork!

There was no acknowledgement that assessment through observation takes time and planning, and must be done during sessions when the child is present. There was also little acceptance that these records should be used to inform planning. As there was no National Curriculum to shape judgements, the schedules matched the curriculum taught in the individual setting or school, and the records were difficult to transfer to another school or nursery.

What this method looks like now

Now we have a National Curriculum in each of the countries of the UK, we have national expectations for children at different stages of development, and a common framework for assessment. There is no longer a need for settings and schools to 'knit their own' assessment schedules, although of course the format for recording *is* still a decision for the individual setting.

The 'Let's screen everyone' model

This sort of assessment was often inspired by a manager or enthusiastic practitioner, or even a whole local authority, where there was a particular interest in finding out about reading, language development, spelling, or in compiling statistical evidence about groups or cohorts of children. There was a surge in the production of screening tests that could be used for whole groups or across a city or county, and these could be used, marked and analysed by schools and settings or the local education authority (LEA) themselves, rather than referring individual children to specialists. The statistics were often used to support applications for additional funding and to identify areas of deprivation or particular need.

The problems

The main problem with these screenings was that they were often used inappropriately across whole groups of children, where many didn't really need to be screened. There was pressure from national and local government departments to collect statistical data, and this tended to be their main use. There was sometimes a problem getting educational psychologists and other agencies to accept the results of these screenings as valid measures for individual children.

What this method looks like now

There have been two major influences on screening – one is that in the UK we now have national assessment procedures for the early years; the other has been the huge leap forward in identifying and responding to individual needs. The special needs Code of Practice and all the recent work on inclusion have raised practitioners' awareness of the individual child and the ways in which their needs can be met. Every child is now assessed in the early years using the framework of the curriculum and the outcomes of this universal screening can now be used to assist learning for every child, and to support referrals for those whose development does not fall within the expected range.

The 'Not sure where we fit' model

When the National Curriculum was first implemented in England, Reception aged children (those aged four to five), were included in Key Stage 1, and were subject to the same programmes of study and assessment arrangements. Assessment and record keeping focused almost entirely on preparing children for the Year 1 programme. Schools also got very interested in baseline assessments, particularly once inspection got going, as they were keen to establish 'added value' or progress models which recognised starting points, particularly in areas of social deprivation or mixed ethnicity.

The problems

Reception teachers suffered from a 'top down' pressure on both the curriculum and assessment, and for them, doing two major assessments in one year put huge constraints on teachers and children. This often resulted in inflated assessment figures, or in providing an inappropriately formal curriculum unsuited to the children's needs and sometimes resulting in under-achievement. Achievements in pre-school and nursery were usually ignored, and baselines started with entry to schools.

What this method looks like now

Fortunately, in England, the government realised that Reception aged children needed a curriculum suited to their stage of development, and this should be in closer alignment with other early years settings. They implemented first the *Desirable Outcomes on Entering Compulsory Education* (1996), a schedule for assessing children as they reached compulsory school age. This set of indicators was fairly rapidly superseded by *Birth to Three Matters* (2002) for children from birth to three years old and *Curriculum Guidance for the Foundation Stage* (2000), which included the Early Learning Goals for children aged four and five. Finally *The Early Years Foundation Stage* (2007/8) stitched together early years provision and assessment for children from birth to 60+ months.

Each of these frameworks had their own assessment guidance and banks of statements for assessment. The EYFS has formative assessment criteria in the Development Matters statements and summative assessment in the EYFS Profile. The other countries within the UK have also recognised the importance of coherent guidance across the whole range of early years experience. Although each variation may cover different parts of provision and periods of development, they all recognise the importance of assessment through observation, using clear criteria.

The future

Who knows what will happen in the next few years? Assessment will be with us for as long as the professionals who work with children in their early years are interested in them as individuals, in watching them and 'catching them in the learning process'. It will remain while there are practitioners who are genuinely interested in what young children know and can do now, what they are interested in knowing and doing, and how they, as adults, might help the child to do this.

> 'Adults have a crucial role in stimulating and supporting children to reach beyond their current limits, inspiring their learning and supporting their development. It is through the active intervention, guidance and support of a skilled adult that children make the most progress in their learning. This does not mean pushing children too far or too fast, but instead meeting children where they are, showing them the next open door, and helping them to walk through it. It means being a partner with children, enjoying with them the power of their curiosity and the thrill of finding out what they can do.'
> *Learning, Playing and Interacting: Good practice in the Early Years Foundation Stage*
> (Department for Children, Schools and Families [DCSF], 2009)

Assessment is a fascinating, time-consuming activity, one that is a central responsibility of all practitioners. I hope the following chapters may help you to make assessment an enjoyable, manageable and useful part of every day.

Introduction

Where did all this focus on assessment come from?

At the heart of any curriculum is the learning process. When children learn, they are constantly restructuring the connections between brain cells, making new links, reinforcing old ones, and pruning those that have ceased to be relevant. This process is both fascinating to watch (even from the outside) and extremely difficult to capture, particularly in the early years when brain-building is at its most complex and rapid. This is the reason why observation is the most important way to collect information, and that observations should be a daily component of planning and review of our work.

Professional assessment measures

Assessment is the attempt to capture and quantify a process, and is an activity undertaken by all conscientious professionals. Doctors assess what is wrong with their patients through diagnosis, and how well they recover or manage their illnesses and conditions; advertisers assess how well their work promotes the products and services of those who employ them; builders assess the quality of their building methods and materials. A growing number of organisations and government led bodies use professional assessment measures to evaluate effectiveness in all areas of government spending.

Of course, many of these measures of success used in reports and the media are of 'outcomes', sometimes measured against externally set targets e.g. How many people recover fully from operations? How many prisoners re-offend? How many children achieve the expected levels for their ages? How many bottles of shampoo have been sold? How much household waste has been recycled? These simple outcome measures are used to evaluate (and sometimes criticise) projects, businesses, manufacturers and individual performance all over the world. They are widely reported in the media and in research, particularly when making comparisons or reporting problems.

Early years programmes

Early years provision across the world has been under particular scrutiny and constant development during the past 50 years. Governments have been exploring and investing in the links between future achievement in education, a successful economy, social indicators such as crime/unemployment, and the quality of early years provision. Intervention programmes, funded by governments have sprung up across the world. These have a universal intention of enhancing the years before statutory schooling, supporting parents, and providing out-of-home pre-school care of high quality and maximum educational and social impact. Exploring the purposes and progress of some of these programmes makes interesting reading:

Head Start was initiated in the USA in 1965, with the intent to '*promote school readiness by enhancing the social and cognitive development of children through the provision of educational, health, nutritional, social and other services*'. The programme has now been in place for more than 40 years, and has attracted world-wide interest.

A whole range of schemes based on the Head Start model are now supported in countries across the world, and these include **Sure Start**, now running across the UK, with an aim of '*giving children the best possible start in life*'. At the other end of the world, the **Te Whariki** ('a mat for all to stand on') early years curriculum, is a more recent government initiative in New Zealand introduced in 1996 with the aim for children '*To grow up as competent and confident learners and communicators, healthy in mind, body, and spirit, secure in their sense of belonging and in the knowledge that they make a valued contribution to society*'. Even though it is such a recent innovation, Te Whariki is recognised world wide as a successful and well-documented approach where 'Learning Journeys' form the central part of assessment.

There are other education programmes based on individual philosophies, such as those of Rudolph Steiner or Maria Montessori; or in research into the way young children learn, such as High/Scope in the USA and the Reggio Emilia schools of Italy. These originally functioned independently of government funding, and some remain entirely in the private sector. However, others now receive some funding from governments, and are as accountable for standards as those in the state sector. In England, any early years school or setting (including those in the private sector) can now apply for funding under the Nursery Education Grant provision for children under five, as long as they follow the National Curriculum for the early years (the EYFS) and assess children's progress towards the Early Learning Goals (ELG) and the EYFS Profile.

In the UK, as in many other countries, early years provision has become both a way of raising educational standards, and a way to engineer social change by improving both the education of children and the parenting skills of their families.

Programme success

The long-term success of Head Start programmes is still becoming evident 40 years after the original programme was devised. The change in children's futures has influenced politicians throughout the world who also wish to raise standards and to reduce the effects of social pressures on the poorest children. Impressive outcomes, collated in 1990, indicate that children who attended Head Start programmes, relative to their siblings who did not, are significantly more likely to complete high school, attend college, and possibly have higher earnings in their early twenties. They are less likely to have been booked or charged with a crime, and are more likely to have successful personal relationships. The educational outcomes of the programme are less well agreed, as there is some evidence that although there are significant benefits early on, the initial advantage of the programme is not sustained, and siblings who did not attend the Head Start programme soon catch up once they start school.

Of course, government funded early years programmes cost a great deal of taxpayers' money. They aim to provide high quality support and education, and with such expenditure inevitably there is accountability – usually in measures of improved outcomes matched to expenditure, or 'value for money'. These rely almost entirely on the collection of evidence through assessment by teachers and practitioners who know the children well.

The process of assessment

In 2002, when Tony Bertram and Chris Pascal undertook a review of early years provision in 20 countries across the world, they came to the following conclusions about the process of assessment in the early years:

> 'In most cases the assessment was achieved through the use of systematic teacher observation and scrutiny of the child's portfolio of activity.
>
> However, the use of ongoing assessment of children by class teachers and carers throughout the early years as a formative strategy for curriculum planning was almost universal. In most cases this was actively encouraged at national level as a signal of good practice. This continuous, formative assessment was generally achieved through the use of a range of informal strategies, including observation, developmental checklists, videotapes, portfolios of children's activity, discussion with parents and the children themselves. Mostly, they were implemented and used at setting level, and formed the basis for curriculum planning and feedback reporting to parents.'
>
> *'Early Years Education: An International Perspective'*, Tony Bertram and Chris Pascal
> (Centre for Research in Early Childhood, Birmingham UK, 2002)

This combination of assessment tools (systematic observation, coupled with scrutiny of portfolios of children's activities in photos and other recorded evidence) was and still is the most appropriate and the most effective way of finding out what

Catching them at it!

children know and are able to do. That is why the notion of 'Catching them at it' became the focus and the title of this book.

Every government-funded initiative is supported by written guidance on philosophy and practice, programmes of learning, and assessment frameworks and procedures. In the UK, government-driven systems have resulted in the Early Years Foundation Stage in England, The Foundation Phase in Wales, The Curriculum for Excellence in Scotland and the Foundation Stage in Northern Ireland. They all have clear guidance on the value and process of assessment in the early years.

Defining observation and assessment

In England, the guidance contains helpful definitions of observation and assessment, and makes explicit the link between these and planning for learning.

> 'Observation, assessment and planning all support children's development and learning. Planning starts with observing children in order to understand and consider their current interests, development and learning.
>
> *Observation*
> Observation describes the process of watching the children in our care, listening to them and taking note of what we see and hear.
>
> *Assessment*
> We assess children's progress by analysing our observations and deciding what they tell us. We also need to find out about children's care and learning needs from their parents and from these we can identify the children's requirements, interests, current development and learning.
>
> *Planning*
> We plan for the next steps in children's development and learning. Much of this needs to be done on the basis of what we have found out from our own observations and assessments as well as information from parents.'
> *The Early Years Foundation Stage* CD-ROM (DCSF, 2008)

It is gratifying to professionals that most governments, when evaluating the success of early years programmes, are now promoting assessment for learning, even though some are still tempted to take too much notice of simplistic data resulting from 'end of early years' summative assessment. We must thank the persistence and idealism of those education advisers close to governments for using their influence to secure the place of formative assessment through observation at the heart of their guidance to practitioners, and it is formative assessment, currently referred to as 'assessment for learning' (AfL) that will occupy the following chapters of this book.

Assessment for learning

'Assessment is the process of analysing and reviewing what we know about children's development and learning – for example, what we observed.

We need to ask ourselves: what does our observation and any other evidence of learning we have collected (such as examples of the child's mark-making, information from parents, a photograph we took or video recordings we have made) tell us about the child's learning and development? What was new – something we had not observed before?

When we do this regularly we have evidence of children's progress over time and we gain insights into children's learning, development and their needs.

Effective assessment involves evaluation or decisions about the child's progress and their learning and development needs and gives us the information we need to plan for the next steps. This is called assessment for learning: it is the formative assessment, based on observations, which informs or guides everyday planning.'

Effective practice: Observation, Assessment and Planning
The Early Years Foundation Stage CD-ROM: (DCSF, 2008)

In the rest of this book, I will be attempting to unscramble assessment for learning in the early years. This is the most complex sort of assessment – the assessment of <u>process</u>, where adults who work with young children look at learning in action, and then use the information to recognise successes and plan for the next steps.

'It is more than simply giving marks or grades, although that may well be a part of it. And because it involves making a judgement it will almost inevitably include an element of subjectivity by the assessor. However, we should strive to make assessment as objective, fair and transparent as possible.'

'Basic Assessment Issues and Terminology', Chris Rust,
Oxford Centre for Staff and Learning Development, 2002

This sort of assessment gives us the most useful and valuable information but it is also the most time-consuming to collect and interpret. Young children are constantly on the move, both mentally and physically, and they are engaged in active learning which is notoriously difficult to pin down. Children know and can do things one day, then seem to have forgotten the next. They can demonstrate skills with one adult, but not with another. They use language at home that they seem unwilling to use in our settings and they behave in totally different ways with different children, in different places and even in different weather conditions!

Keys to the assessment process

Practitioners and those who advise them know that there is a way of finding out what children really know and can do, and some of the keys to this process are:

- Observing children systematically in a range of places and situations, and particularly in child-initiated play where children really show what they can do.

  'Observation of children participating in everyday activities is the most reliable way to build up an accurate picture of what children know, understand, feel, are interested in and can do.' *Early Years Foundation Stage Profile Handbook* (DCSF, 2008)

- Providing an environment where children can follow their own interests and practise the skills and activities that are important to them, not just to us; and being open to surprises and new learning, not just the objectives we have identified as adults.

  'Judgements against these scales should be made from observation of consistent and independent behaviour, predominantly from children's self-initiated activities.' *Early Years Foundation Stage Profile Handbook* (DCSF, 2008)

- Talking with children about their play and learning, asking questions, helping them to understand what they have learned, and what the next steps are for them; involving them as genuine partners in their learning.

  'Talk helps children to understand what they experience. It is important that they have a chance to express their own ideas, as well as have conversations to hear other people's ideas, extend their thinking, and use language about learning.' *Learning, Playing and Interacting: Good Practice in the Early Years Foundation Stage* (DCSF, 2009)

  'The quality of questioning is vital in helping children to become independent thinkers and learners, and to extend their learning.' *Observing Children* (Wales Guidance for the Foundation Phase) (Department for Children, Education, Lifelong Learning and Skills [DCELLS], 2008)

- Involving all the adults in the setting, as well as parents, carers and others who know the child.

  '...all adults who interact with the child should contribute to the process (of assessment) and that account will be taken of information given by parents.' *Statutory Framework for the Early Years Foundation Stage* (DCSF, 2008)

- Collecting examples of learning in action, using a range of techniques, including observation, portfolios and learning journeys, photos, examples of talk and discussion.

'The adult is an interested observer of play, finding out about the individual children and the community that is created through play. The adult should seek to discover what children are interested in, know and can do in order to support their learning more effectively.' *Learning, Playing and Interacting: Good Practice in the Early Years Foundation Stage* (DCSF, 2009)

- Using this information to identify what should happen next, what should be planned, supported, offered or encouraged:

'Practitioners observe children's activities carefully, trying to discover what the child is thinking about and learning and the goals of the play, so they can accurately support and extend the child's learning focus either at the time, or later by changes to the environment or in planned activities.

This does not mean pushing children too far or too fast, but instead meeting children where they are, showing them the next open door, and helping them to walk through it. It means being a partner with children, enjoying with them the power of their curiosity and the thrill of finding out what they can do.' *Learning, Playing and Interacting: Good Practice in the Early Years Foundation Stage* (DCSF, 2009)

Meeting children at that door, and genuinely helping them through it, without 'pushing them too far or too fast' is the job of the skilled practitioners, as well as the central focus of this book.

1   The principles, purposes and audiences for assessment

If learning is so difficult to track, and assessment can give us such unreliable information, why do we do it? This book explores what we *must* do, what we *could* do, and what is manageable for us in our work.

In this chapter I will begin to explore the nature and principles of assessment:

What is assessment? The clear definitions.
Why should we do it? The principles we should stick to.
Who is it for? The central audiences for our assessment work.

What is assessment?

When we talk generally about assessment, we usually encompass three processes – assessment, which is <u>collecting information</u> about learning; <u>recording</u> our assessment findings so we can make judgements about what has been learned and what needs to happen next; and <u>reporting</u> judgements to others. If we get the first two parts of the process right, the third will be both easy and useful.

Most assessment systems emphasise the key role played by observation in making the process reliable and useful:

'Observational assessment and record-keeping involve building up a manageable picture of what a child knows, understands, feels and can do in order to:
* plan the next steps in development and learning;
* plan the provision to enable these next steps to be successful (formative assessment);
* help children as they are learning (assessment for learning);
* mark staging posts in a child's and groups of children's development and learning (summative assessment);
* evaluate the impact of the quality of provision, environment and the level of practitioner training on development and learning (assessment of the conditions for learning).

The impact of observational assessment is not measurable by its weight. It is the use to which the practitioner puts their observations that is important.'

Creating the Picture (DFES, 2007)

Here is one description of observation and how it can contribute to the assessment process:

- 'Observation is the formal term for one of the most important aspects of day-to-day professional practice when working with children of all ages.
- It is how we find out the specific needs of individual children by carefully looking, listening and noting the activities of a child or group of children.
- Observation allows us to see a child as an individual; this is important for every child in whatever setting but even more important in large group settings.
- Observation should be both formal (planned) but much of it will be informal (spontaneous) carried out as you work with the children.
- Without observation, overall planning would simply be based on what we felt was important, fun or interesting (or all three) but it might not necessarily meet the needs of the children in our care.
- Carrying out regular observations is vital because it ensures that we put the child at the centre of our practice.
- We can discover what new skills and abilities emerge over time through observation. For example when a baby is able to sit up steadily, or a young child can pour their own drink, think about somebody else's feelings, assign meanings to the marks they make on paper, or ride a bicycle without stabilisers.
- Observation enables us to identify each child's likes and dislikes and their responses to different situations such as care routines or new people.
- We can find out which experiences, routines or activities a child seems to enjoy or to find difficult and any that seem to make them anxious.
- Observation helps us assess children's progress; we can find out about the specific care and learning needs of each child. We can then plan next steps in children's learning.'

Effective Practice: Observation, Assessment and Planning
The Early Years Foundation Stage CD-ROM: (DCSF,2008)

This useful document contains a process diagram, also included in much of the more recent guidance for the early years curriculum:

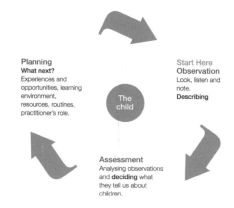

Planning
What next?
Experiences and opportunities, learning environment, resources, routines, practitioner's role.

The child

Start Here
Observation
Look, listen and note.
Describing

Assessment
Analysing observations and **deciding** what they tell us about children.

Catching them at it!

So what is the connection between observation and assessment, record keeping and reporting?

This diagram helps to clarify the three elements of assessment, recording and reporting, and is purposely divided into three unequal sections.

Assessment

More space, time and attention is, and should be, paid to the collection of evidence (Assessment for learning or AfL) almost entirely through observation, than to recording or reporting which condenses the information into easily understood documentation.

Recording

Drawing together these observations and other information and noting what this is telling us (recording in individual records or trackers) is a periodic activity, done perhaps every month or half term.

Reporting

Reporting is the final activity, undertaken every year (or sometimes more frequently, on change of school, for identifying progress against targets, or for seeking additional support for individual needs). This activity is selective. It dips into the rest of the process and selects key information to present for a particular purpose or audience. This smallest, most selective part of the process cannot give the depth or detail of the information on which it is based, and this is sometimes frustrating when misinterpreted.

Paul Black and Dylan William have worked in the field of assessment for learning for many years and their work, including 'Inside the Black Box' (2001) and 'Formative Assessment: Promises or problems?' (2007) has been very influential in defining and improving assessment in the classroom. This work has focused on schools (they use 'teacher' and 'student' in this work). However, their principles and definitions are also helpful to those of us who work in the early years. Here they define assessment, and how, in order to become 'formative assessment', the information must be used to adapt teaching to meet needs:

> 'In this paper, the term 'assessment' refers to all those activities undertaken by teachers, and by their students in assessing themselves, which provide information to be used as feedback to modify the teaching and learning activities in which they are engaged. Such assessment becomes 'formative assessment' when the evidence is actually used to adapt the teaching work to meet the needs.'
>
> *'Inside the Black Box: Raising standards through classroom assessment'* Paul Black and Dylan William, King's College London School of Education (2001)

Black and William have also clarified the difference between assessment for learning, with its focus on promoting children's learning, and assessment primarily used for 'accountability, ranking or certifying competence':

> 'Assessment for learning is any assessment for which the first priority in its design and practice is to serve the purpose of promoting pupils' learning. It thus differs from assessment designed primarily to serve the purposes of accountability, or of ranking, or of certifying competence.
>
> An assessment activity can help learning if it provides information to be used as feedback, by teachers, and by their pupils in assessing themselves and each other, to modify the teaching and learning activities in which they are engaged. Such assessment becomes 'formative assessment' when the evidence is actually used to adapt the teaching work to meet learning needs.'
>
> *'The Nature and Value of Formative Assessment for Learning'*, Paul Black, King's College London School of Education (2004)

Children in the early years are active and inquisitive. They don't always learn things in a predictable order, and they show their learning through their faces, bodies and voices, not by writing answers to our questions or by doing homework that can be marked. They also change during the day and the week, learning, forgetting, misunderstanding, connecting, practising and revisiting the things they are learning, piecing together the experiences they have each day, and sometimes making their own sense of what they have learned. Young children often appear to understand, appear to be able to do something, appear to know stuff which we subsequently realise they have only partly grasped.

One thing practitioners learn very early in their work is that what may be described in books as an organised 'learning spiral' or web is in fact a much more complex process, more like the saying 'two steps forward, one step back, or even one step sideways' as the child revisits and reorganises pathways in their brain.

Catching them at it!

'No matter how meticulously we plan or what marvellous strategies we use during teaching, we can't reach inside learners' heads and put the learning there. There is a gap between learning and teaching that learners have to negotiate in order to construct new knowledge, skills and attitudes – albeit with our skilled input and help. We can't put learning in their heads!'

> *Assessment for learning: A Practical Guide* (Northern Ireland Curriculum);
> (The Council for the Curriculum, Qualifications and Assessment [CCEA], 2009)

Assessment in the UK

So, with the implementation of national frameworks for the early years in all four constituent countries of the UK, how is assessment described in early years guidance in these countries and how do these compare with countries across the world?

The EYFS guidance for England defines assessment as:

'Ongoing assessment is an integral part of the learning and development process. Providers must ensure that practitioners are observing children and responding appropriately to help them make progress from birth towards the early learning goals.'

> *Statutory Framework for the Early Years Foundation Stage* (DCSF, 2008)

The guidance on assessment in the Foundation Phase (three to seven) in Wales says:

'It is essential that practitioners working with children have an understanding of child development and the needs of children. By observing children carefully to note their progress, involvement and enjoyment, as well as focusing on the attainment of predetermined outcomes, practitioners should be able to plan a more appropriate curriculum that supports children's development according to individual needs.'

> *Observing Children*, (DCELLS,2008)

In Northern Ireland:

'It is important to view learning, teaching and assessment as a continuous cycle, where assessment is not the end point but should feed back into the process to help to improve learning. Since the purpose of teaching and the main purpose of assessment are to help children to learn, teaching and assessment need to be planned together as complementary aspects of the one activity. In turn, the information obtained from assessments should be used to inform the planning process.'

> *Understanding the Foundation Stage* (Northern Ireland) (CCEA, 2006)

and in Scotland:

'Assessment involves gathering, reflecting on and evaluating evidence of learning to enable staff to check on learners' progress.'

Curriculum for Excellence, Building the Curriculum 5:
A Framework for Assessment (The Scottish Government, 2010)

In all of these examples, observation is at the heart of, and at the start of the assessment process and has a key influence on planning. The repeating daily, weekly and annual cycle of assessment and planning is at the centre of both learning and teaching in the early years, as this diagram explains:

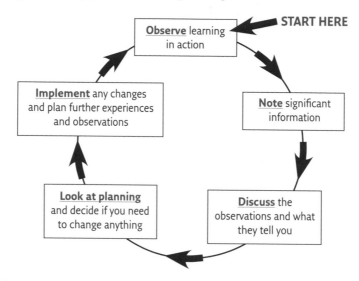

The central guiding principle of assessment is that any assessments must be both *useful* and *used*. If we put this principle into action, our daily observations inform the next day's planning and provision; our weekly and monthly collections of evidence inform our medium-term planning, and of course our long-term consideration of children's learning, through annual reviews, reports and children's portfolios will influence our planning, organisation and provision for the following year.

The guidance for the Scottish Curriculum encapsulates this process in the following aide-memoir:

'Assessment needs to be planned as part of learning and teaching activities. In planning activities and experiences with young people, staff need to:
- consider and share the outcomes towards which children and young people are working

- use examples that illustrate standards and expectations
- agree success criteria through discussion with each other and with learners
- design learning experiences and activities that are likely to challenge and motivate and give opportunities to children and young people to provide evidence that demonstrates their knowledge and understanding, skills, attributes and capabilities
- plan so that children and young people can show their thinking and provide evidence of what they have learned in response to planned experiences.'

Curriculum for Excellence, Building the Curriculum 5:
A Framework for Assessment (The Scottish Government, 2010)

Assessment across the world

Across the world, assessment systems for the early years have common messages. Here are some examples:

High/Scope settings use assessments developed for their own curriculum, and described in this way:
'With these tools, teachers, administrators and caregivers can monitor each child's developmental progress, plan appropriate daily activities based on observations recorded in anecdotal notes, and communicate effectively with parents and other important decision-makers about children's achievements.' *www.highscope.org*

In Reggio Emilia schools in Italy:
'Much attention is given to detailed observation and documentation of learning and the learning process takes priority over the final product. It is a model that demonstrates a strong relationship between educational establishment and community and provides a remarkable programme for professional development.'
(Quote from Learning and Teaching Scotland)

In Te Whariki, the early years curriculum for New Zealand:
'These (assessment) criteria are: having clear goals, balancing the documented and the undocumented, siting assessment in everyday contexts, protecting and enhancing the motivation to learn, acknowledging uncertainty, listening to children, including collective assessments, and keeping a view of learning as complex.' *www. educate.ece.govt.nz*

Clarification of the definition of assessment should lead us to thinking about the principles on which we base our practice in observing and assessing children's learning or asking why should we do it?

The principles we should stick to

Principles are often the bit we skip over when reading or writing guidance for learning and teaching, but they are essential tools for checking why we are working the way we are, and how well we are doing it. Assessment principles need to be agreed within each school or setting. Even if we discuss and then decide to adopt an existing set of principles such as those contained in local or national guidance for the early years, discussion within the team confirms a shared commitment and helps to establish a coherent approach to the process.

Sometimes the principles for assessment are stated within an overall statement of curriculum principles, such as these from High/Scope:

> 'The five basic principles – active learning, positive adult-child interactions; a child-friendly learning environment; a consistent daily routine; and team-based daily child assessment – form the framework of the High/Scope approach.'
>
> *Educating Young Children: Active Learning Processes for Preschool and Childcare Programs*; Mary Hohmann and David P. Weikart (High/Scope Publications, 2002)

These overarching but simple principles guide all the work in High/Scope settings and schools, giving everyone a framework for their practice.

As in High/Scope, national guidance for the early years curriculum in countries throughout the world always makes mention of assessment, often amplified in specific principles for assessment in separate documentation on assessment. For instance, the EYFS in England has several volumes of guidance on assessment, rooted in the following eight assessment principles.

I have followed each of the principles with some questions to lead your thinking and your team's discussion of practice in your setting:

1. **Assessment must have a *purpose*.**
   Points to think about: Are our assessments purposeful? Do we know **why** we are doing them? Who and what are they for?

2. ***Observation* of children participating *in everyday activities* is the most reliable way to build up an accurate picture of what children know, understand, feel, are interested in and can do.**
   Points to think about: Do we make most of our assessments through observation? Do we have a clear system to make sure we observe every child regularly? Do we observe activities that the children have really chosen for themselves?

3. **Observation should be *planned*. However, practitioners should *also be ready to capture spontaneous but important moments*.**

Points to think about: How well do we plan for assessment, so we are not feeling under pressure? How much time do we allocate to watching children? How systematic is our observation process? What is the balance between planned observations and capturing spontaneous moments? How do we use the observations to help with planning?

4. **Judgement of children's development and learning should be based on** *skills, knowledge, understanding and behaviour that they demonstrate consistently* **and** *independently.*
   Points to think about: Are most of the observations of child-initiated activities done frequently? Can we be sure that our assessment of each child recognises evidence from different activities, in different places and with different companions?

5. **An effective assessment will take into account** *all aspects of a child's development and learning.*
   Points to think about: Does our assessment programme recognise all aspects of the child and the curriculum? Do we recognise and include particular strengths and interests of individuals? Are we truly focusing on the 'whole child'?

6. **Accurate assessment will also take into account** *contributions from a range of perspectives.*
   Points to think about: Do we include contributions from all colleagues – teaching assistants, nursery nurses and officers, representatives from outside agencies such as speech therapy and so on?

7. *Parents and other primary carers should be actively engaged* **in the assessment**
   Points to think about: Do we include and value contributions from parents and carers?

8. *Children should be fully involved* **in their own assessment.**
   Points to think about: Do we include and value contributions from the children themselves?

Take a moment to think about some of the assessments you make in your work, and look at them with these principles in mind. How well are you doing in your setting? Can you identify the things you are doing well?

Clear principles help practitioners to make the assessment process both manageable and meaningful for adults and children, providing useful information, which is well used to shape future experiences – an essential key to successful practice. Any assessment you make should give you useful information, which contributes to the picture of the child that you are gradually building up. However, if you don't use the information you have collected, you are wasting time collecting it! Every time you plan an assessment activity, ask yourself these two key questions:

Does this assessment give me useful information? *And* do I use this information to improve the provision for the child?

Here are some examples of how the balance can vary between 'useful assessment' and 'assessment properly used'. How would you respond to each of these examples?

Example 1: A practitioner collects pages of information from parents at pre-admission home visits. She carefully copies her notes onto a form and files them in a beautiful ring binder in her cupboard and never refers to it again. This potentially useful information is NEVER used!

Example 2: Another practitioner is asked by her manager to use the EYFS profile statements to assess the three year olds in her group. These assessments are scrutinised by the manager who creates complex charts of 'progress made' and 'attainment' for each child. Using an assessment schedule intended for five year olds to assess the learning of three year olds does NOT provide useful information, but it is used as if it did!

Example 3: A group of practitioners in a pre-school frequently make mental notes and jottings as they work and play alongside the children. At the end of every day they meet and discuss the significant things they have seen, and what they might do on the following day to improve their provision. These are USEFUL assessments, professionally USED.

Who is assessment for?

As mentioned earlier in this chapter, assessment needs clarity in both the <u>purpose</u> (in the principles and processes) and <u>audience</u> (the feedback to children and adults). We have to know why are we assessing and who it is for.

As you will see from the principles for assessment, there has been an increasing emphasis on involving colleagues, parents and carers, and children themselves in assessment activities.

'Contributions from a range of perspectives including the child's and should be drawn from all adults who have significant interactions with the child...these may include records and any formal or informal discussions with adults involved with the child'

and

'Parents and other primary carers should be actively engaged in the assessment process...(and)...children should be fully involved in their own assessment'

Early Years Foundation Stage Profile Handbook
(Qualifications and Curriculum Authority [QCA]. 2008)

Of course, children and their parents are the key audiences in our day-to-day assessment processes, but, when we consider all the information, we discover a whole range of groups needing to be both involved and informed about assessment. These fall into the following broad groups:

- children
- parents, carers and families
- practitioners in the setting or school
- managers and heads of settings and schools
- governors of schools
- outside agencies such as therapists and special needs services
- local authority personnel
- inspectors
- local and national government.

It is possible, but not always easy, to give all these groups a sense of involvement in the <u>process</u> by listening carefully and involving them in the setting.

It is quite another thing when you consider the <u>outcomes</u> of assessment. Each of the groups needs different sorts of information, presented to them in ways they can understand. Parents need and want information about their own child, in language they can understand, and years of research has shown that they are centrally interested in two things – 'Is my child happy?' and 'Are they getting on as well as they could?' Local and national governments are particularly interested in simple statistics that describe cohort (year group) or school/setting averages and general standards. Inspectors are interested in both the process and the outcomes of assessment, and as their visits are now so brief, they need this in easily digested form.

It is easy to forget that children need feedback too, and a sense of involvement in how they are doing, and this principle is at the heart of assessment for learning. Children need support and praise for success, but they also need opportunities to stop and think about what they are learning, and helpful feedback on where they are and what they need to do to improve. As one teacher put it:

'The children's minds are focused on what they are learning, especially during play-based learning, when we pause between activities and ask "Can anyone tell me something new they've learned?"'

Assessment for Learning: A Practical Guide (CCEA Northern Ireland, 2009)

And of course practitioners need the whole picture. Their job is to resist assessing just because they have been told to, or filling out returns to managers or government agencies because it is required, but instead they should <u>use</u> the information from every observation or assessment they make to improve provision, involving everyone in the process, not just the outcomes. Nobody has ever tried to pretend that the job is easy, and the more you try, the more difficult it seems to be to get the whole process right for everyone.

Here are some examples of the work of practitioners, some is principled assessment, some is less so. As you read the examples, ask yourself 'Who are these assessment processes for?'

Are they for the children, the adults, for both or no-one?

- Rory (age four) is involved in taking regular photos of his work and the activities he likes. Once he has taken the photos they are printed by his key worker who sticks them in his record book, but never discusses them with him. Rory is never involved in talking about why he takes the photos, what they tell him or other people about his choices, or what he might do next with these favourite resources.
- Keran (age four) also takes photos regularly. He downloads them onto the computer, prints them himself, shows them at group sessions and tells the other children why he took them. He puts some of them in his virtual portfolio (a computer based collection of photos for each child, sometimes annotated with his own words, typed in by a practitioner) and takes others home, where he can discuss his activities and progress with his parents.
- Kelly plans an activity for her key group for group time every day. She matches the activities carefully to children's interests and abilities. When the activity is complete, Kelly sends the children off to play and then writes notes about what has happened during the activity. She uses these to plan the next day's work.
- Meena plans activities for her key group. As she works with the children she gives them frequent feedback about what they are doing, asking open questions, giving clear praise for success and making notes on her notepad as she works. At the end of the session she makes time to talk to the children about what she has written, talking with them about what went well and how the children could develop or improve their skills. She involves the children in deciding what they need to do next, and plans this for the next day.

Are they for the practitioners, the parents or the children?

- In Matthew's setting, practitioners use sticky notes for jottings down things they notice during the day. They put these in individual children's files at the end of the session, and visit each child's page after the children have left, as they check that what they have planned for the next day is still meeting the needs of the children. The discussion includes informal observations, which have not always been written down. These indicate children's current interests, schema play and changing friendships. The next morning, the files are available for parents to read if they wish, and many do. A pack of sticky notes is placed near the files, so parents can comment too.
- In Sarah's setting the sticky notes are carefully linked to the six areas of the curriculum. These are also put in individual children's files, but informal observations are not discussed and the files are not available for parents to look at. Parents' comments are not included in day-to-day assessment, although they are always asked to comment on their child's annual report.

Are they for the managers or the practitioners?

- At the beginning of the year, Cara is asked by her manager to produce targets for numeracy and literacy for each of the children in her Reception class, using the end of year statements in the curriculum (the EYFS Profile). The manager checks progress against these targets each half term, using samples of children's work and her own observations, and then produces a chart of progress against the targets, which is used as part of Sarah's Performance Review. Sarah does not refer to the targets between annual performance reviews.
- Marta assesses each child in her Reception class during the first two weeks of the autumn term. She uses these assessments to set simple targets in three areas of learning – 'talking and listening', 'getting on with others', and 'using numbers'. These targets are discussed with the children, and each child has the targets in the front of their workbook, which they use for all their recorded work. Marta sends copies of the targets to each child's parents, with an invitation to discuss these if they wish. She also gives a copy to her team leader, and keeps another in her planning folder to help with grouping, with her planning, and with differentiating activities. Marta also refers to the targets regularly as she observes the children and talks to them. When a target is met, there is celebration in the class and at home. Targets are reviewed formally every half term and renewed or adjusted according to each child's needs.

Take a bit of time to think about how each of these practitioners has responded to the need for everyone to know what is happening. Involving everyone is a time-consuming and sometimes frustrating job, but well managed it can be very rewarding and can result in better learning and better teaching.

A final comment from a teacher about the benefits for parents of real understanding of assessment:

'Parents are much more likely to react positively to changes in feedback and assessment arrangements in schools if they are informed about and understand the educational rationale behind them.'

Assessment for Learning: A Practical Guide (CCEA Northern Ireland, 2009)

2 Assessment in practice – the nuts and bolts

Once we have our principles agreed, and we have identified our audiences we can begin to unpick the practicalities of assessment, the daily and weekly decisions about making space, time and energy for the process and for following the educational leads it presents us with.

Further chapters in this book will explore in more depth the 'how' of assessment, by identifying a range of ways of assessing learning, from informal observation which may not even be written down, to formal tests such as those used to identify children's additional learning needs. Here I will refer to the broad range of tasks around the timing, planning and methodology of the whole assessment process, including recording and reporting.

When is assessment done?

If we return to the diagram in the previous chapter, we can now begin to add some details to the process.

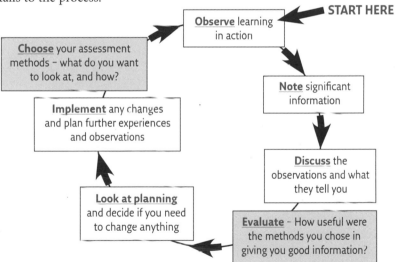

START HERE

Observe learning in action

Note significant information

Discuss the observations and what they tell you

Evaluate – How useful were the methods you chose in giving you good information?

Look at planning and decide if you need to change anything

Implement any changes and plan further experiences and observations

Choose your assessment methods – what do you want to look at, and how?

It is easy to overlook the 'how' and 'when' stages of the process, assuming that we can find out everything we need to know about learning by one method, or that everything is fine when we only look at a small proportion of what is going on. It is also very tempting to think we will find time to observe and assess children's learning without actually allocating time for it in our day and week.

Consider these examples:

- **The baby room:** the practitioners in the baby room wanted to give the children more individual choice of the toys and other resources in the room, instead of putting out the toys they thought the babies would like. They decided to monitor the gestures and 'eye pointing' of individual children, giving the babies any toy they indicated. This seemed to give the babies many more opportunities to choose the toy they wanted, and most of them seemed much happier and played for longer with their chosen toys.

    However two babies still seemed unhappy and restless until one practitioner said 'It's no good just letting them choose from the ones they can see, some of the toys are in the cupboard. I know Jamie really likes the musical toys and he can't see them!' This comment, based on informal knowledge of a child in her key group helped all the staff to understand that babies may need to be carried round the room, including looking in open cupboards so they can have a genuine choice of all the toys on offer.

- **The book corner:** Julie and her Reception team wanted to know why the book corner was under-used during free choice time. They looked at all their observations and found that they had very little information about the use of this space. They decided to systematically observe the use of this area, but knew that if one of them went to sit there, children would automatically come too! They decided to use a more subtle method of observation. They drew up an observation schedule, and Julie looked up every five minutes from whatever she was doing to jot down who was in the book corner and what they were doing.

    After a few days, the team looked at the information and found that far from being under-used, the book corner was visited by the majority of children over these days, although they sometimes didn't stay very long. The practitioners decided to ask the children what would make the book corner more inviting and comfortable for a longer stay. The children really enjoyed being involved in the improvements, and the result was that they really did stay longer.

- **ICT experiences:** Laura has a key group of three and four year olds, and she wanted to check their experiences of ICT. She made a list of all the equipment, such as the photocopier, digital camera, light box, computer and so on. She added a picture of the equipment to each item on the list, then called the children to her one at a time, asking them if they knew what each one was and how to use it. Most of the children were able to name the equipment, and some could explain in words and gestures something about how to use it, but it didn't give Laura much evidence of the sorts of experiences they had had or the skills they had acquired.

    When she had talked to four of the children she decided that the information she was getting was of no real use to her, so she stopped using this method and planned to set up some specific activities with ICT equipment that she could observe and photograph in action. This gave her much more useful information, and she was able to discuss the activities with each child, getting even more information, including their use of and understanding of technical language.

The practitioners' stories told above all describe professional attempts to 'capture' the effectiveness of their provision. Each one has given time and thought to what they are doing, and we would recognise their commitment to the process.

So how do we choose the methods and plan the time for that crucial observation of children, particularly when they are engrossed in activities they have chosen themselves?

Ten tips for assessment

Managing the process of assessment, day-to-day and week-by-week is central to its success. Here are *ten tips* for making the process manageable when you are planning for assessment, with some excerpts from guidance to expand each one:

Tip 1: Commit yourselves

Make a team commitment to observation, write a small statement of intent, such as:

> *We all know the importance of observing learning, and we commit ourselves to a balanced programme of written observations and informal assessment by other means such as discussion, taking photos, listening to children talking etc. This will ensure that every child's strengths and interests are recognised, and their achievements across the whole curriculum are acknowledged.*

If you have made a commitment in writing, you are much more likely to keep to it.

Tip 2: Know your percentages

This version of our original assessment triangle clarifies the percentages generally agreed to be relevant when observing young children.

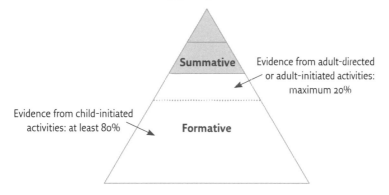

When government guidance on assessment within the EYFS was first circulated, practitioners asked what *consistent*, *independent* and *predominantly* mean in the following statement,

> 'Judgements ... should be made from observation of consistent and independent behaviour, predominantly children's self-initiated activities.'
>
> *The Early Years Foundation Stage* (DCSF, 2008)

The response from the government was clear:

> 'Practitioners need to ensure that no more than 20% of the total evidence for each scale point is gained from (adult-led and adult-initiated activities). The remainder of evidence should be drawn from knowledge of the child, observations and anecdotal assessments. Practitioners are neither expected nor required to create onerous systems in order to demonstrate this, but need to be aware of this ratio when considering the evidence to finalise their EYFS profile judgements.
>
> 80% of evidence needs to stem from knowledge of the child and observational evidence of child-initiated activity. Only 20% of evidence can be gathered from adult-directed or focused assessments.'
>
> *Early Years Foundation Stage Profile Handbook* (QCA, 2008).

This clarification of percentages helped practitioners to understand where the majority of their observations should take place. It has also caused some practitioners to revisit their planning and the management of their time, as some had previously taken advantage of children's enthusiasm for their own interests to concentrate on adult-led group work, to read with children or to work with those who have additional learning needs. The most effective assessment happens when you concentrate entirely on being with the children during child-initiated learning periods.

Learning, Playing and Interacting: Good Practice in the Early Years Foundation Stage (DCSF, 2009) has helpfully explored this tension, the powerful nature of child-initiated learning, and how practitioners can enhance children's experiences by their presence as they observe self-initiated activities.

> 'The adult should seek to discover what children are interested in, know and can do in order to support their learning more effectively. Children's achievements across all areas of learning can be recognised through observing play.
>
> Practitioners plan adult-led activities with awareness of the children in the setting and of their responsibility to support children's progress in all areas of learning. They will build on what children know and can do, and often draw on interests and use materials or themes observed in child-initiated activities.'

Tip 3: Know your stuff and balance your methods

There are many ways of observing and recording learning, and of giving feedback to children on how they are doing. You will already know some of them. See pages 72–80 for a description of many more, and the advantages and disadvantages of each. Remember to always ask yourself 'Why am I doing this, and what do I want to find out?' – this is principled assessment. Some of the time (but not more than 20 per cent) you will want to collect evidence through adult-led tasks and activities.

'At one end, too little adult support can limit learning. While play without adults can be rich and purposeful, at times it can become chaotic or repetitive activity, which is 'hands-on, brains-off'. At the other end of the scale, too much tightly directed activity deprives children of the opportunity to engage actively with learning. Effective Early Years practitioners will organise the time, space and activities in the daily routine to reflect the overall combination which best supports children's well-being and learning.' *Learning, Playing and Interacting: Good Practice in the Early Years Foundation Stage* (DCSF, 2009)

Tip 4: Make time

It has been said that if you are not spending at least 20 per cent of your time with the children in assessment activities, then you are not doing enough assessment. This figure (the equivalent of one day a week) seems horrific, but before you put this book down and go rushing around in a panic, remember that there are a huge number of activities that constitute assessment. You are 'doing assessment' when:

- you ask a child a question and listen carefully to the answer
- you check with a parent to confirm that a young child is consistently using her left hand at home as she is at nursery
- you make a note to check again the child who doesn't seem to be understanding the concept of 'more and less'
- you ask your colleague to work with a small group of children who appear to be having difficulty using scissors
- you share a book with a child, encouraging them to take turns with you in reading
- you join a group of children in the construction area, working alongside them, and observing how they are working.

All these, and many more are assessment activities, take up time even when you do them on a professional 'autopilot' as many multi-tasking professionals do. Most practitioners are observing and assessing progress with part of their brain during the whole session, and many are almost unconsciously adjusting what they do in the light of what they see. Of course it would save a lot of time if we could do all our assessment work in the background as we do other things, but time spent in close observation, noting what we see and discussing this with others is one of our most important professional activities. When we give time to observations, we sometimes feel:

– guilty that we aren't 'teaching'
– harassed when we never have enough time to do everything anyway
– or *as if we aren't doing our jobs properly* when we are sitting with a clipboard, talking with children, or just looking at how things are going.

We *must* stop feeling guilty, and support each other in this vital part of our role. It is vital to set aside parts of the day when you will be consciously and systematically gathering evidence of children's learning. These will include being clear about what an observer is expected to do (a job description for observers!) and making sure you include these elements in your planning:

● planned observations of individual 'focus children'
● allowing time at the end of adult-led activity sessions to jot down significant information
● arranging for your colleague to observe particular children as you lead plenary or group times
● producing and trying out simple schedules for tracking activities or individuals
● giving significant time to 'longer recorded observations' of activities, individuals or groups
● identifying objectives or intentions from your long or medium-term planning which you intend to observe
● observing and providing for children's emerging interests
● talking with individuals and groups.

Tip 5: Acknowledge when things aren't working

This might, for example, mean realising that your presence in an activity is altering the behaviour of the children; discussing whether doing all your observations on the same day of the week is giving you information on all the children, or abandoning a simple schedule that is easy to fill in, but gives no useful data. A vital professional activity is looking at what you are doing, and making sure it is an effective use of your time.

Tip 6: Look for the learning, not just what you expect

If all your planned observations and assessments are carefully focused on individual objectives (or intentions), it is very tempting to ignore all the other information that the children are offering you. Be open to other information, note this as well as what you planned or expected. Use the time to look broadly, while not forgetting your original focus. This takes practice, it is easy to get distracted!

Tip 7: Share the load

Observational assessment is very time consuming, so it is vital to use everyone to help with this important job. Everyone in the setting can and should be involved. Practitioners (teachers, teaching assistants, nursery nurses and nursery officers) all have a real contribution to make, particularly because they can give a new perspective on the child or the activity. Students, volunteers, parents and other visitors often see your setting in a different light and can make useful comments on what they see. And of course, the children themselves can open our eyes to what is important to them.

Tip 8: Be out of doors as well as inside

Observations of children in the outside area, and on walks, trips and visits will give you a new view of what interests them, what they can do and who they like to play with. These observations will enable you to value the whole child; and for some children, the outdoors is the only place where they can really be themselves.

Tip 9: Know and note what's significant

It is easy to spend a lot of time writing down everything you see, or what a child is doing for every minute. Looking carefully for what is important (significant) in what you see is an art, and takes time to learn. One practitioner described this as 'instant editing'. She follows the advice 'watch for five minutes, then write what is significant about what you have just seen'. This helps her to focus and distill what she is seeing.

> 'It is obviously not possible to record everything a child says or does, even in a very short period, however it is desirable to record the important aspects of the situation observed. The significance of any situation will be determined by the adult's previous knowledge of the child.'
>
> *Understanding the Foundation Stage* (CCEA, 2006)

Tip 10: Follow the children

When you are observing child-initiated learning, don't be tempted to say 'I'll go and watch Bonnie in the home corner'. Bonnie will almost certainly decide not to go to the home corner, or to leave it as soon as you arrive, so it's important to be flexible and follow them. Otherwise, how can you possibly know what you need to do next?

How is assessment used?

At the beginning of this chapter I recommended that assessment should be both useful and used. This statement might seem obvious, but asking yourself why you do observations, ask questions or set challenges for children is an important part of the job. Assessment is not only important in accountability to the government or your managers, it has a vital contribution to make to the job of an early years practitioner.

Assessment can also be used to:

- **Feedback to individuals**
  An example: *Martha told the children at group time that she had seen Garry and Shaun doing something very interesting, using chalk to make up a monster counting game on the stepping-stones in the garden. She invited the boys to tell the other children about their game and how to play it. Next day, several other children joined the boys in their game. Martha joined in too.*

  Assessment information is most useful when the key findings are fed back appropriately to the person who is being assessed. This does *not* mean you have to feed back every observation to every child, but you should be building in some reference to your observations when you discuss activities with individuals and groups.

- **Ensuring the curriculum is meeting the needs of the children**
  An example: *Paula was observing a small group of children in the garden, using the scale point 'Selects and uses resources independently' as her focus. She could not find much evidence for this scale point, and soon realised why. The adults put all the equipment out for the children, and controlled their use of it by strict rota systems. The children couldn't access the equipment independently, only when the adults told them it was their turn. She recommended to the other staff that they should find a way of letting the children have more freedom to select and use the resources independently.*

  Assessment should help you to see if the activities and resources you are offering to the children help them to learn the things you want them to know.

- **Ensuring you are meeting the needs of every child in your group, particularly those with additional needs and children who have English as an Additional Language (EAL)**
  An example: *The manager of the nursery asked Clare to observe a new child with EAL to check that he was getting access to a range of activities. Clare observed him over two days and found that despite his limited English, he was in fact getting involved in a whole range of activities, even though he could not always make himself understood.*

Assessment should give you information about children with additional needs, and how you are meeting them.

- **Enhancing opportunities for learning**
  An example: *Caran and her colleagues spent a day looking at whether the resources for play in their setting gave children opportunities to find out more about pirates (their current centre of interest) during child-initiated time. They watched role-play, games outside, the book corner, the workshop and mark-making areas to check. They found that children were using the role-play resources and the pirate books to extend their ideas about pirates, but there was no use of the workshop and mark-making areas.*

  They decided to draw children's attention to the objects pirates use (telescopes, treasure chests, treasure maps etc) and to offer some suitable resources in the mark-making and workshop areas to stimulate their interest. They added cardboard tubes, pictures of treasure maps, boxes for treasure chests, gold foil and other items to the existing resources. Further observations showed that the new resources had inspired children to expand their play and the way they used all the areas of the room.

  Observation helps you to find out whether children are using the resources you are offering to reinforce and extend knowledge and skills through their current interests.

- **Monitoring teaching and learning**
  An example: *Paul was responsible for the fine motor skills development of the children in the nursery. He regularly checked their progress by planning and observing an adult-led activity, such as cutting along a line, threading beads, picking up small objects with tweezers, finger painting and so on. He logged children's progress on a simple tick sheet to indicate whether they could do the task easily/with some difficulty/with great difficulty/not at all. He used the observation evidence to plan further fine motor skills practice in self-initiated and adult-led sessions.*

  Assessment information is useful in deciding whether what you are planning and teaching is what children are learning!

- **Tracking children's activities and interests to find out who is doing what, and when**
  An example: *Four weeks after she moved into her group, Maddy's key person, Shelpa, was updating the children's records. She found that she had less information about Maddy than the other children in her group, and felt that she didn't know Maddy's interests and friends very well. So Shelpa spent a day tracking her by logging where Maddy was and what she was doing every 15 minutes. Maddy was not aware of Shelpa. When Shelpa looked at the tracking information, she found*

that Maddy spent most of her time alone or on the edge of groups, watching the other children. Shelpa decided to join Maddy sometimes, to help her to enter play situations and make friends.

Assessment information should give you information about how individuals use the resources and activities you offer.

- **Monitoring the use, access and participation in activities, resources and spaces**

An example: *The practitioners in a pre-school felt that the girls were not choosing to play with the blocks or in the construction area. They talked about whether this was important, and agreed that block and construction play could offer opportunities that other areas of the setting could not. Firstly they watched the children informally and found that their impression was right, girls rarely chose to play in these areas. They tried an experiment. They put a box of play people in the block area, and took turns to join construction play, modelling how a female could build and construct too.*

Assessment can give you information about whether the activities you offer are being accessed by all the children. We sometimes assume that if we plan or offer something, all the children will experience it.

'Ongoing observation, carried out in a range of contexts and across the areas of Learning and Development, will be the key way of assessing children's needs in EYFS. The approaches used for young children should align with what is required by the EYFSP (formative assessment during the final year of the EYFS, often a reception class). The systems and approaches used must grow from the needs of the very youngest children; they should not be watered-down versions of approaches appropriate for older children.'

Creating the Picture (DFES, 2007)

Of course, we could get so obsessed with assessment and spend so much time doing it that there is no time left to teach! Effective settings and effective professionals work hard to get the balance right between teaching and learning and assessment, making sure that they plan enough time for assessment, but not too much. These effective practitioners are very clear about what they *must* do (because it is the law) and what they *could* do to set the legal requirements in an assessment framework that is really useful to everyone.

An exploration of the legal requirements comes in the next chapter, and is followed by chapters on assessment and recording methods.

3 | What are my legal responsibilities?

What are the requirements?

The *requirements* are those things that practitioners in the early years in each country or each education system *must* do. They are enshrined in law, in employment contracts and in the conditions attached to local or national government funding. Relevant legislation for safeguarding children's welfare when they are out of their parents' care is set down in national documentation, along with the legal requirements for the curriculum and its assessment.

In England, these are all collected and neatly presented together in the *Statutory Framework for the Early Years Foundation Stage* (DCSF, May 2008). Any statement including the word 'must' is likely to be a legal requirement, and is underlined when used. Those statements containing the words 'should' or 'might' (also underlined in the following text) are likely to indicate guidance on something practitioners and settings could do if they wish, or are advised to. Some of this guidance is generated in local government (local authorities in England) and is intended to help practitioners to interpret the legislation. Of course, guidance is intended to be helpful, but some of it, including some of the 'should/might' statements, makes the guidance seem more like requirements. It is important to be clear about what you *must* do and check it regularly!

In general requirements are things that a practitioner must do:

1. because there is **legislation that affects everyone in the country**, such as health and safety, equality of opportunity, anti-discrimination, or employment law;
2. because the **government** requires those who work with children to do them if they work in the state education system;
3. because **their employer** requires their employees to undertake them if they work in a private or independent nursery or school;
4. or because **their employer has accepted a state regulation** as a condition of receiving state funding or grant aid.

Because early years provision in the UK, and particularly in England, is so diverse, the requirements for assessment, recording and reporting in England fall into all these groups. They are compulsory for practitioners who work in state funded education provision and are a condition of receiving Nursery Education Grant in the private, voluntary and independent sector. The requirements in England are described here in brief. The full versions appear in the EYFS documentation and other government guidance on assessment, recording and reporting. If you work in another country in the UK or abroad, you will need to be clear about your own responsibilities, as there will be variations.

In England, information about the requirements for the curriculum and for assessment are set out in four areas:

- · the curriculum entitlement for every child *and*
  The requirements for:
- assessment
- recording
- reporting to parents and carers, including the information sent to the next school or setting.

For ease of reference, the assessment, recording and reporting requirements for England are presented here in sequenced sections:

1. The requirements for assessment during the EYFS – from birth to five years.
2. The requirements for assessment at the end of the EYFS (the end of Reception year, the year in which the child becomes five and transfers to statutory primary school education).
3. The requirements for record keeping during the EYFS.
4. The requirements for annual reports to parents during the EYFS.

1. The requirements for assessment during the EYFS

These requirements are from the *Statutory Framework for the Early Years Foundation Stage* (DCSF, 2008). The first quote includes a statutory requirement as well as some guidance on how it should be met:

'2.19 Ongoing assessment is an integral part of the learning and development process. Providers <u>must</u> ensure that practitioners are observing children and responding appropriately to help them make progress from birth towards the early learning goals. Where practitioners require additional training in order to assess capably and objectively, it is the responsibility of the provider to ensure practitioners receive the support that they need. Assessments <u>should</u> be based on practitioners' observation of what children are doing in their day-to-day activities. As judgements are based on observational evidence gathered from a wide range of learning and teaching contexts, it is expected that all adults who interact with the child <u>should</u> contribute to the process, and that account will be taken of information provided by parents. An essential feature of parental involvement is an ongoing dialogue, building on the partnership begun by any previous practitioner(s). Settings <u>should</u> report progress and achievements to parents throughout the EYFS.'

During the early years, the requirement is simply that practitioners must observe the children and respond to what they see, so they can help children make progress. There is no requirement for how much time should be spent on observation; how much should be written down; how much the parents should be told and when, how or even whether the observation evidence should be kept. The requirement is just that, between birth and five, observations should be used to help children make progress towards the goals for early learning.

The next paragraph in the document gives explanatory guidance on what the requirement might look like in practice (note the use of 'should'):

'2.20 The *Practice Guidance for the Early Years Foundation Stage* sets out detailed formative assessment suggestions in the 'Look, listen and note' sections of the areas of Learning and Development. Practitioners <u>should</u>:
- make systematic observations and assessments of each child's achievements, interests and learning styles;
- use these observations and assessments to identify learning priorities and plan relevant and motivating learning experiences for each child;
- match their observations to the expectations of the early learning goals.'

Again there is no requirement to record the observations. However, the documentation does go on to give us some guidance in the following sections on what that process might look like (my précis of the text):

- all practitioners in the setting <u>should</u> be involved in the process
- systematic observations <u>should</u> be made in a wide range of contexts and day-to-day experiences
- planning <u>should</u> build on experience at home and in previous settings
- parents <u>should</u> be kept informed throughout the early years
- observations <u>should</u> be matched to the expectations of the early learning goals (and the 'Development Matters' statements)
- observations <u>should</u> be used to plan future learning experiences.

So, during the EYFS, there is a single legal requirement for assessment –'Observe, and use your observations to help children make progress'.

How practitioners do this is up to the setting to decide, using any guidance they care to seek.

2. The requirements for assessment at the end of the EYFS

These requirements are from the *Statutory Framework for the Early Years Foundation Stage* (DCSF, 2008). The EYFS is now a statutory stage of the National Curriculum for England, and as such is bound by the same legislation as state (maintained) schools.

'2.21 The EYFS Profile is a way of summing up each child's development and learning achievements at the end of the EYFS. It is based on practitioners' ongoing observation and assessments in all six areas of Learning and Development. Each child's level of development <u>must</u> be recorded against the 13 assessment scales derived from the early learning goals. Judgements against these scales, which are set out in Appendix 1, <u>should</u> be made from observation of consistent and independent behaviour, predominantly children's self-initiated activities.

2.22 Some children will have experienced a range of settings during the final year of the EYFS and may have a number of carers. In these cases the EYFS Profile must be completed by the provider where the child spends the majority of time between 8 am and 6 pm. Providers <u>should</u> take account of all available records and of any formal or informal discussions with the parents and with those involved with children in the previous year.

2.23 Children with special educational needs may be working below the level of the scales and require an alternative approach to assessment. In these cases providers <u>may</u> use the assessment systems of their local authority or other systems according to the needs of the children.

2.24 At the end of the EYFS providers <u>must</u> ensure that children are assessed against the 13 scales in the EYFS Profile. Providers may use the e-Profile (available from local authorities) or their own record keeping systems (see below). Regulations made under Section 99 of the Childcare Act 2006 require early years providers to provide information about the assessments they carry out to local authorities. Local authorities are under a duty to return this data to the DCSF.

2.25 Local authorities have a duty to monitor and moderate the EYFS Profile judgements to ensure that providers are making assessments that are consistent across settings. Providers <u>must</u> take part in these arrangements.'

Electronic data collection and submission tools

'There are several systems available (including eProfile) that enable the recording of assessments for individual children at scale point level. They facilitate voluntary electronic submission of this level of data in addition to the statutory collection of total scale point scores. EYFS providers and local authorities may use any system as long as it enables practitioners to complete a profile summary of scores in each of the 13 assessment scales for every child at the end of the EYFS.'

Assessment and Reporting Arrangements 2011: Key Stage 1 (ARA) (QCDA, 2010)

The assessment and recording guidance does make a requirement that practitioners should record (write down) their judgements at the end of the Foundation Stage, and gives some guidance on what the process might look like.

Practitioners must:

- Complete the EYFS Profile for each child in the final term of the EYFS (and no later than 30 June). This should be done by the provider where the child spends the majority of time between 8 am and 6 pm.
- Use the EYFS Profile to sum up observations from the whole of the EYFS, over all six areas of learning and development.
- Ensure that judgements are made from observation of consistent and independent behaviour, predominantly children's self-initiated activities.
- Take account of all available records and discussions with parents.
- Use alternative methods for assessing children who may be working below the levels of the scales in the EYFS Profile.
- Record a level for each against the 13 scales of the EYFS Profile.
- Provide access to the assessment process and recorded information to local authorities, who must submit data to the government.
- Take part in reasonable moderation activities.
- Provide for parents:
  - a written report which summarises the child's progress against early learning goals and assessment scales;
  - a copy of the EYFS Profile if parents want it;
  - details of when and where the report can be discussed with the practitioner.
- Provide for a new setting or school:
  - any Profile data collected;
  - the provider's assessment of this;
  - if no Profile has been completed, the reason why not.

. . . .

So, at the end of the EYFS, the requirements are that practitioners must:
- **within the final year of the EYFS, use the EYFS Profile to assess every child (taking into account the detailed requirements of this process)**
- **provide the results of this assessment to local and national government and to the next provider or teacher**
- **within the final term, provide a written report to parents on the progress of their child (taking into account the detailed requirements of this process).**

. . . .

3. The requirements for record keeping during the EYFS

The detailed guidance and regulations vary a little across different parts of the early years sector receiving Nursery Education Grants (including maintained schools) in England. The simple messages are:

Personal records

'Providers <u>must</u> maintain records, policies and procedures required for the safe and efficient management of the settings and to meet the needs of the children.

Providers <u>must</u> record the following information for each child in their care: full name; date of birth; the name and address of every parent and carer who is known to the provider; which of these parents or carers the child normally lives with; emergency contact details of the parents and carers.

Providers <u>must</u> record and submit the following information to their local authority about individual children receiving the free entitlement to early years provision as part of the Early Years Census: full name; date of birth; address; gender; ethnicity;* special educational needs status; the number of funded hours taken up during the census week; total number of hours (funded and unfunded) taken up at the setting during the census week.

*This data item can be collected on a voluntary basis. A child's ethnicity should only be recorded where parents have identified the ethnicity of their child themselves.'

Statutory Framework for the Early Years Foundation Stage (DCSF, 2008)

Providers <u>must</u> allow parents access to see their child's records, if they request it.

Curricular records

In addition, early years providers who are part of maintained schools (but NOT maintained Nursery Schools) <u>must</u>:

Ensure that a curricular record is kept for every pupil registered at the school and update it at least once every school year. The governing body is responsible for this requirement.

Respond to parents' requests to see or have copies of their child's educational record.

The educational record will include the curricular record but also other information about the pupil that <u>may</u> be kept by the school, such as details of behaviour and family background.

The Education (Pupil Information) (England) Regulations; 2005

Catching them at it!

Reception teachers

What records are Reception teachers required to keep?

- a record for every child, including the key information about each child;
- update this record at least once a year;
- include a curricular record and other relevant information, but NOT the notes teachers keep for their own use;
- add a copy of the most recent report to parents;
- keep the records safe and secure;
- share these records with parents and make copies available if requested;
- send relevant information to the local authority;
- keep copies of the records in a secure place 'for a reasonable time' after the child has left (for schools this period is three years).

Remember:

It is for schools to decide:
- the best way to mark work and record progress (this will depend on the children's particular needs)
- how much evidence and which records to retain – as a guide, schools should keep enough information to help them plan future work (this is all that Ofsted inspectors will need to see).

Assessment and Reporting Arrangements 2010: Key Stage 1 (ARA) (QCA, 2009)

. . . .

So, the requirements for record keeping are that practitioners must keep a record for each child and update it every year. Then during the final year of the EYFS, use the EYFS Profile to assess every child, record the outcomes and report these to parents and others.

. . . .

4. The requirements for annual reports to parents during the EYFS

Settings for children who are not in maintained schools <u>must</u> report regularly to parents, but there is NO requirement for this to be a written report (although many settings do report in writing).

Reporting during the EYFS is *not* a requirement, although many pre-schools and other early years providers provide written reports and copies of EYFS Profile information if they complete the Profile in their setting.

Annual reports to parents in the final year of the EYFS (the Reception Year) and beyond

The Law in England
Schools *(but not nursery schools)* <u>must</u> give parents a written report on their child at least once a year. This <u>must</u> include:

- progress on all the National Curriculum subjects (or areas) they have studied
- progress in other subjects and activities
- general progress and attendance
- results in any National Curriculum tests and assessments (including the EYFS Profile).

Assessment and Reporting Arrangements 2011: Key Stage 1 (QCDA, 2010)

. . . .

So, what would that look like?
- **All settings must report regularly to parents, throughout the EYFS.**
- **Settings where children are subject to the EYFS Profile, and Reception classes in schools are legally required to report in writing at the end of the Foundation Stage on the outcomes of the EYFS Profile.**

. . . .

Exploding some myths

Should I be writing down everything I observe?
There is no requirement to write down what you observe during the Foundation Stage. It is up to you to decide what is significant, what to write down or record in other ways, and what to keep. It is important to discuss and agree with your colleagues how much evidence to collect, and what form it should take.

How much evidence should I keep?
It is up to you to decide how much you keep, but once you have recorded your judgements on the child's record, you do not need to keep all the evidence. It is important to discuss and agree with your colleagues how much evidence to keep after regular record keeping.

How much time must I spend on assessment?
There are no requirements for how much time you should spend on observing learning, the format your observations should take, or how often you should do them.

What should our personal records look like?
The format for records is for the setting to decide, although there are some requirements on things it must contain. Records can be paper based or electronic.

Do I have to update 'official' individual records every half term?

There is no requirement to do this more than once a year, but most practitioners do update some sort of record about once a half term to help them to keep the curriculum on track, and to make sure individual children don't get missed. If your informal records can give you all this information, and if your manager agrees, you could follow the requirement and only update records once a year, but this would be unusual.

What should our reports to parents look like?

It is up to the setting to decide, and there is no requirement for a written record for children until they are in their final year of the EYFS. Many settings, however, do report in writing every year, and there are many formats available on the Internet to help you decide on your own.

Do we have to keep children's records for ever after they leave? We have nowhere to store them!

No, the guidance is that you should keep them for three years. This is a reason for making them manageable, or consider secure electronic storage!

> There is some confusion about the regulations relating to children who remain in the Private, Voluntary and Independent sector for the Reception Year, and the EYFS Profile is completed in these settings. The Assessment and Recording Arrangements 2011: Key Stage 1 (ARA) (QCDA, 2010) clarifies this, and includes a table of information as Appendix 3.

Some guidance on record keeping

Here are six principles for record keeping (the written information resulting from assessment by observation). They are included in EYFS guidance in England, and are followed by some points that you could discuss in your setting.

1. **Record keeping must be meaningful and have a purpose.**
   Have we discussed the purposes of our record keeping? Do we feel it makes a real contribution to children's learning, or is it just a chore?

2. **The task of keeping records must be manageable and sustainable.**
   Have we invented a time-greedy monster? Can we sustain the model we currently have?

3. **Records must capture the range of children's attainment, achievement and progress.**
   Do our records really celebrate the whole child or do they lean towards literacy and numeracy, allowing important areas of interest and learning to take second place (or no place at all)? Do we include all the areas of learning identified in our planning?

4. **Records will reflect the individuality of every child and the diversity of their backgrounds.**

How much time do we spend finding out about the children as individuals, and where does this knowledge feature in what we say about them and how we value their learning and their culture?

5. **All significant participants in children's development and learning should contribute to the information gathering.**

Do we include contributions from colleagues – teaching assistants, nursery nurses, nursery officers and other professionals? Do we include parents and children in recognising and celebrating achievements as partners, not just as an audience for our judgements?

6. **Records should be shared with the child.**

Do we genuinely share both assessment and record keeping with the children, making them partners in the learning process, understanding what they do well and what they need to do next? How do they contribute to the process?

Guidance in the rest of the UK

The other countries in the UK have also produced guidance on assessment and reporting to support their most recent versions of early years curriculum documentation.

Universal access across the UK to pre-school education is a recent development for us all, and the four governments have responded in different ways, on different time-lines, and with differing emphases. Their guidance on assessment has a common theme of observation, their development of 'end-of-early-years' assessments has progressed at different rates, and in some of the countries in the UK such assessments are still in development. However, readers who work in other countries or other school systems may find the following information of interest in exploring the wider implications of recording and reporting children's achievements:

The Foundation Phase in Wales (age three to seven)

'The information that has been collated should be used in future planning and to inform parents/carers of the children's progress.

Some information will be needed in the short term while some will need to be kept for the longer term. It is important that any form of recording is not burdensome for staff and that the amount of paper is kept to a minimum.

The type and range of record-keeping to assist with practitioner assessment is a matter for settings/schools to decide. Elaborate arrangements for recording and retaining evidence of assessments are neither required for Foundation Phase

Catching them at it!

assessment purposes nor necessary to satisfy Estyn inspection requirements.' (ESTYN is the Inspection system in Wales) *Observing Children* (DCELLS, 2008).

and:

'Teacher assessment covers the full range and scope of the Foundation Phase learning continuum. It should take account of evidence of achievement in a range of contexts, including that gained through discussion and observation throughout the Foundation Phase.

At the end of the Foundation Phase, teachers are required to assess and report outcomes attained by each child by means of teacher assessment in:
- Personal and Social Development, Well-Being and Cultural Diversity
- Language, Literacy and Communication Skills in English or Welsh
- Mathematical Development.'

Framework for Children's Learning for 3 to 7-year-olds in Wales (DCELLS, 2008)

The Foundation Stage in Northern Ireland (age three to five)

'Observations are a natural and essential part of good practice for teachers and classroom assistants. Without the use of regular observations and written records on each child's development, the teacher is left with an incomplete picture of the child. This may lead to the loss of significant information that could help shape planning and take more account of each child's needs.'

Understanding the Foundation Stage (CCEA, 2006)

The Curriculum for Excellence in Scotland (age three to sixteen)

'For monitoring and tracking to be successful, records of children's and young people's achievements and progress need to be manageable. Staff should use assessment information from a wide range of sources to monitor learners' progress and plan next steps in learning. Assessment information should be shared and discussed with the learner, parents, other staff as appropriate, and partners involved in supporting learning. All can contribute at appropriate times to setting targets for learning and ensuring appropriate support for each child and young person.'

Curriculum for Excellence, Building the Curriculum 5:
A Framework for Assessment (The Scottish Government, 2010)

and:

'From time to time teachers also take stock of their learners' progress and achievements in order to be able to plan ahead and to record and report on progress. This is vital in ensuring that learners' progress is on track and that action is being taken to address any problems at the earliest possible point.

This taking stock relates to broad standards and expectations, for example deciding whether a level for a curriculum area, or part of an area such as reading, has been achieved or what additional learning and support is needed.

It involves teachers in evaluating a range of evidence produced over a period of time to provide a summary of progress and achievement, including for qualifications and awards. It can be carried out in a number of ways, including by weighing up all relevant evidence, taking account of the breadth, challenge and application of learning.'

Curriculum for Excellence, Building the Curriculum 5:
A Framework for Assessment (The Scottish Government, 2010)

Education legislation in any country or system will change over time, each time education law changes, so you need to keep up with the changes that affect you. In England information is published annually which lays out the regulations and guidance on assessment, including any changes to legislation. It is vital to keep up with documentation such as this, because some legislation changes very quietly!

Now the regulations are out of the way, we can continue to explore how to assess in a way that is helpful to learning, and how to create and keep manageable records.

Catching them at it!

4 Assessment methods, the good the bad and the plain pointless!

Assessment for learning is like cooking, it is great to have lots of recipes, but some become favourites, and can become so familiar that we can cook them without thinking, and without asking ourselves whether they are 'fit for purpose'. Every so often, just like a chef, we need to refresh our memories about other ingredients and recipes.

This chapter is intended as a resource for you and your colleagues, a collection of assessment methods for you to dip into as you work. There are many different ways to assess learning, and I have tried to include as much of the range as I can, although any collection will inevitably have gaps.

When you are selecting methods of assessment, it's vital to keep the principles in mind, and particularly those associated with the following:

- Is it <u>reliable</u>? – can I really count on the information? Does it really show me what the child can do?
- Does it give <u>useful</u> information? – will the information be in a form that I can use? Will we use it?
- Is it '<u>time efficient</u>'? – is the information gathered by this method worth the time invested in doing it? Have we planned enough time to do it?

Here are some of the methods we have at our disposal, with their advantages and disadvantages. If you need more ideas about how your assessments can be recorded, see pages 72–80, where the range of ways of recording is explored.

Observation methods

Observation (informal or participant observations)

All humans use informal observation to make hundreds of assessments of other people every day. Parents, practitioners and teachers use these informal observations to assess how well children are developing. The information often enters our memory without conscious effort, and informs our opinion of the person we observe and what they can do.

> 'Participant observations are observations you note down while you are fully involved with the children, noting down significant things you see. Although this might be most of what you observe, it is important that some observations are planned, so that time is set aside for you to watch the children at play. You will need to focus on what one child is doing, including in this the interactions she(he) has with others around. This type of observation often allows you to gather a different type of information about how the child is responding to your setting than when you are carrying out a participant observation, as you will see what the child chooses to do independently.'
>
> Effective practice: Observation Assessment and Planning
> *The Early Years Foundation Stage* CD-ROM (DCSF, 2008)

Advantages

Informal observation just happens, it's like osmosis, and happens often without the observer being conscious of what they are doing or seeing. These observations build gradually into a complex picture of the child, most of which is not written down.

Disadvantages

This sort of observation is random, and the picture of the child may be skewed because of this. In a class or group, some children may not be observed as much as others, or may be observed over a narrow range of activities, times of day or locations.

Observation (formal)

These observations are built into the day or the week. They can be long or short, but they have a clear focus. This focus may be a single child, a group, or 'focus' children. The observation could also be of an activity or skill, an area of learning, or a particular place. The focus can be 'loose' or 'tight', with room for manoeuvre if the focus or activity changes or develops. Planned observations are usually recorded in writing, photo sequences or other recordings. The recommendation in the EYFS documentation is that:

> 'These planned observations usually last for anything from between three and ten minutes. Very occasionally they may be longer if resources allow.'
>
> Effective practice: Observation, Assessment and Planning
> *The Early Years Foundation Stage* CD-ROM (DCSF, 2008)

Catching them at it!

Advantages

Practitioners find planned observations useful in ensuring that they observe every child over a range of activities throughout the year, and that the curriculum provision is systematically covered.

Disadvantages

Once a focus has been decided, it can be difficult to accept children's own agendas, or to register additional information that is not related to the original focus.

Comparative narrative

A comparative narrative can be a written account of two children of the same age at the same time, or of the same child on two different occasions. It is often used to monitor the development of children with additional needs. You could also use this method to quickly assess whether two children are making the sort of progress you expect. In these observations, it is particularly important not to compare the children with each other, just with objective criteria.

Advantages

Observing two children at once can be a more efficient use of time. Observing one child on more than one occasion and comparing the things you find out will make your assessments more reliable.

Disadvantages

It is easy to get distracted watching one child and not give equal time to the other, possibly missing important elements of their learning. It's also difficult to keep your view objective and keep your focus on a manageable number of clear criteria.

Assessment tasks

Assessment tasks are activities planned by the adult, and usually carried out in adult-directed situations, often in small groups. The tasks may be formal, with concrete outcomes, such as models, pictures or writing/mark-making, or informal, with a specific challenge set for the children. The activity is observed by the adult who keeps a record of what happens.

Advantages

The systematic nature of this sort of assessment gives it an element of standardisation where children can be compared to each other and to national, local or school/setting/cohort norms. It can reduce the variables associated with more informal observation.

Disadvantages

Assessment tasks can be rigid and formal, relying on outcomes rather than process. Because the same activity is often used across a group or class, it may lack relevance to individual children's interests and they may not perform as well as they could in an activity they choose themselves.

Tick sheet or checklist

These assessments are often used as a quick check in a group of children on a single criterion (colour/number/letter recognition, handedness, pencil grip) or single activities and skills (can cut along a line, can dress and undress unaided, can build a tower of three bricks). Sometimes these are recorded during adult-directed activities. At other times they are completed during free play or other times when the children are using the focus skills.

Advantages

They are quick and easy to record.

Disadvantages

They can only be used with clear 'yes/no' answers, and only show evidence at a single moment in time.

Snapshot observation

This is a quick and useful way of monitoring what is going on, what an individual child is doing or how children are using the different areas of the setting. Making regular snapshot observations can help you to see which children regularly use the area or activity, those who never do, and how friendship groups are developing. The observer makes notes of who is doing what, whether any children are 'drifting' and any area that is overcrowded or under-used.

Advantages

Snapshot notes are useful when evaluating whether your organisation and activities are meeting the needs of the children.

Disadvantages

One snapshot isn't useful in itself. You need to do this sort of check regularly, and *use* the information to confirm the success of your environment, organisation or planning or to change it.

Tracking

Tracking is a method of following a child, an activity or even a group over time to find out more about what happens. It can also be used to track participation in a particular activity, for example, the writing or block area, or to look at gender involvement. The observer usually decides on a timescale (perhaps every five minutes over a session or even a day) when they will look up from what they are doing and log what the focus child is doing/who is involved in the activity and so on. The record can be made on a plan of the room, by logging the path or track of the child, or in brief notes of what the observer sees. The information can be presented in a time chart, a pie graph or just as a 'trail' on a plan of the room or setting.

Advantages
This assessment can be done alongside other activities, and the observed child is less likely to be aware of the observer. The observation can also give you information over a longer period of time and space.

Disadvantages
The observer needs to be well organised and have a reliable watch or timer. It is easy to forget to look at the right intervals and this may make the observation useless!

Timed sampling

Timed sampling is similar to tracking, but in this method the observer watches the child or children for a set time (one, two or more minutes), then makes notes of what happened during that time, watches for another set period and writes again. The observation can take anything from a few separate minutes to half an hour or more, and can be done in a block or at different times during the day.

Advantages
The observer can watch without having to write at the same time. This often results in better information as the observer does not miss things when they are writing.

Disadvantages
There are no obvious disadvantages to this method of observation, and many early years experts recommend it, particularly for inexperienced practitioners and those who find it difficult to watch and write at the same time.

ABC – reflective event sampling

This method is often used when a child is having problems managing their behaviour. The letters ABC stand for Antecedent (what happened before the event), Behaviour (the tantrum, outburst or other worrying behaviour) and C the Consequence (what followed the event or behaviour). The observations happen every time the behaviour happens to see if there is a pattern or trigger to the problem behaviour. The record continues over sessions, days, or a week, to see if a pattern emerges. The records are analysed to help with behaviour management.

Advantages

ABC offers a way of doing systematic monitoring of the possible triggers in difficult behaviour. This makes it much easier to see patterns, for instance, the trigger may be a particular child, a new situation or even an energy dip just before snack time.

Disadvantages

This sort of systematic observation can be difficult to maintain, particularly when the child is already taking up a lot of your time. It's important to involve everyone, to have a simple way of recording in three columns – A, B and C and to keep the sheets somewhere handy!

Baseline

Baseline assessments are often made when children start at a setting or school, or when they move from group to group. The assessment usually consists of a series of statements, often with yes/no answers. They are sometimes used while discussing the child with their parents or carers or during home or pre-entry visits. Some settings complete these baseline assessments by observing the children during the first weeks in the setting or when the children have had time to settle in.

Advantages

Baseline assessments done through observation in the setting and conversations with parents can be a useful way of monitoring progress at later points in the child's time in the setting, or when they leave.

Disadvantages

Baselines can produce unreliable information, as they are assessments at a critical stage in a child's life, when they may be under huge stress. Some parents see baseline assessments as a test of their parenting, and they may answer in the way they think shows them, and their child, in the best light!

Observation diaries

Some settings make the writing of regular diaries a part of every Key Person's job. This means observing, writing notes, making comments, and taking photos of any other significant events and behaviours for each of the children in their key group. Children with additional needs often have a daily diary, which goes with them from setting to home and back, and parents make comments as well as practitioners.

Advantages

This sort of continuous assessment of progress and learning is a very good way of following a child's progress and is particularly useful in recognising individual interests and in personalising learning. Parents often really like this sort of anecdotal recording, and some settings encourage parents to contribute too.

Disadvantages

Diaries take commitment. Parents love to have regular feedback on what their children are doing. Make sure you don't start on this sort of assessment record unless you can keep it up!

Sociogram

A sociogram is a pictorial or diagrammatic map of the contacts and friendships a child makes during a day or over a period of time. The child's name is in the middle of a page, and directional arrows link them with children who approach them, or who they approach in play. These are best done during free play sessions or child-initiated activities.

Advantages

Social relationships are very important to young children. Recording these over time gives another dimension to your knowledge of the children. It is also a relatively easy way to record information.

Disadvantages

Some very sociable children may spend long periods on their own. Young children make and break friendships very frequently.

Questioning of individuals and small groups

This sort of assessment is often used in plenary sessions, and some practitioners focus on a small group of children each day to get coverage of the whole group and more information about individuals' learning.

'The two main styles of questioning are:

Closed questions, which tend to have a specific focus and usually only allow for one correct answer. Closed questions are useful in:
- ascertaining what children have understood; for example, in a story
- encouraging less-confident children to provide short answers
- acting as a stimulus/springboard for the introduction to extended conversation.

Open questions which tend to be short (sometimes just one word; for example, 'who?', 'when?', 'why?') and provide children with the opportunity to think and discuss a number of possibilities, solutions and ways forward.'

Observing children (DCELLS, 2008)

Advantages (open questions)

Open questions give children the opportunity to think and discuss a number of possibilities, solutions and ways forward. They also allow for an individual response to an activity idea or object.

Disadvantages (open questions)

They are time consuming, and some practitioners find open questions difficult to think of, as most questions they used in the past may have been closed.

Advantages (closed questions)

These tend to have a specific focus and usually only allow for one correct answer. They do have a place as long as we are aware of them. They can be helpful in finding out what children have understood, in encouraging less confident children to contribute, or acting as a stimulus for a longer conversation.

Disadvantages (closed questions)

They do not usually allow for deep thinking on the part of the child.

Longer forms of assessment incorporated in records

Portfolio or learning journey

This is a collection of annotated and dated evidence of the learning and development of one child (photos, comments, observations, pictures and other creations). This portfolio is collected over time, sometimes several years, and is used to celebrate achievements and to provide information for parents and particularly to the next setting or school. Some settings include *all* their assessment information in this folder or file, and see it as the single collection of evidence for each child. Some settings and schools are now collecting information and presenting it digitally in e-portfolios, PowerPoint presentations and other computer based collections.

'The Learning Journey is a continuous journey through which children build on all the things they have already experienced and come across new and interesting

Catching them at it!

challenges. Every child's learning journey takes a personal path based on their own individual interests, experiences and the curriculum on offer.'

Principles into Practice Card 3.2 Enabling Environments: Supporting Every Child
The Early Years Foundation Stage pack (DCSF, 2008)

Advantages
When children are involved in the selection and annotation this is one of the best ways of celebrating the whole child, recognising their individuality and valuing what matters to them.

Disadvantages
The process can be time consuming and some profiles can become very full. This can make the process too cumbersome for transfer, so weeding out and reducing the number of items is important. Electronic collections must be backed up!

Photographs, tape and DVD recordings

Most settings now use photographs to expand their collections of assessment evidence. Some settings also use DVD, video and dictaphone or tape to record children's achievements.

Advantages
Photos and DVD give a good insight into children's learning and make the learning much more visible. They bring real colour to individual experiences and are a reminder to practitioners of what happened.

Disadvantages
This sort of assessment is only useful if it is annotated or transcribed and dated. This can be extremely time consuming.

Case studies

A case study is an in-depth observation of one child over time. It is also a way to collect information about a child who is a cause for concern, or who may have additional needs. Case studies are often undertaken by students, or those in further training, to improve their understanding of child development.

Advantages
Case studies are great for collecting in-depth information about individual children.

Disadvantages
They are time consuming to collect, read and interpret.

Nationally moderated assessment methods

National, age-related assessments

The EYFS Profile and teacher assessment by level at the end of Key Stage 1 are examples of national, age related 'teacher' assessments. In the early years, these assessments are administered by the practitioners in the school or setting, and are used at set points in the school year. They sometimes acknowledge the child's age, and they are used for all sorts of purposes, including measuring the success of teaching. The results are often used out of context and they sometimes take no account of starting points or 'added value' from baselines.

Some independent school systems have evolved their own age-related assessments. The High/Scope series of assessments is an example of this work (see www.highscope.org).

Advantages

They use standard, age-related criteria for whole cohorts, and have detailed guidance on how they should be used. The outcomes can be used to gain information about standards across the school, the local area and the country, and performance of different gender, ethnic or cultural groups.

Disadvantages

Variations in the ways practitioners understand and look for the criteria as they make their judgements can affect the reliability of the findings. Moderation meetings and visits are vital in helping practitioners to make good judgements and come to agreements about evidence.

Tests

Diagnostic tests

These tests are often used when a child is being assessed to diagnose a learning difficulty. They are standardised (the scores are established by using them in very large groups of children) and they usually focus on a narrow band of skills or aptitudes. Some diagnostic tests can only be administered by educational psychologists, therapists, or other staff with responsibility for special needs, because they have specialist skills, impartiality and training in administering, marking and interpreting the results of the tests. They are also knowledgeable in advising on next steps in learning, or strategies for support.

These tests are often administered outside the classroom or setting to preserve the neutral conditions required. Diagnostic tests are also used to establish the needs of gifted children, or to move forward in the process of preparing a statement of special needs.

Advantages
These tests are very specific, and give detailed information to help with diagnosis and support for learning difficulties or gifts. The impartiality of the person administering the test enables them to see the child objectively, something that their practitioner, teacher or key person may find more difficult.

Disadvantages
Tests of this sort only cover small parts of the curriculum, usually those that are the most easily tested or observed. Some practitioners have reservations about testing by a stranger, or outside the secure area of the classroom or setting.

Standardised attainment/achievement tests

These tests measure knowledge and/or skills and are administered in tightly controlled situations. Because they have been standardised over large numbers of children, they can be used to produce a statistical profile in comparison with a national or age-related norm. Reading and maths tests, IQ tests and Key Stage SATs are examples of standardised tests.

The outcomes of these tests have been used to produce statistical information, but this is not always robust because the variables are so wide across practitioner judgements, children and settings or schools.

Advantages
These tests are easy to administer, providing the child can understand the questions! If properly constructed, standardised and marked, they give reliable information and statistics.

Disadvantages
Tests of this sort only cover small parts of the curriculum, usually those that are easily tested or observed. If the curriculum is inappropriately geared to the test, not the programmes of study or the whole curriculum, then children get a limited experience and can be put at a disadvantage in later years. Children who excel in areas of learning that are not easily tested, such as social relationships or the arts can be disadvantaged by these tests.

'Standardized tests can't measure initiative, creativity, imagination, conceptual thinking, curiosity, effort, irony, judgment, commitment, nuance, good will, ethical reflection, or a host of other valuable dispositions and attributes. What they can measure and count are isolated skills, specific facts and function, content knowledge, the least interesting and least significant aspects of learning.'

Bill Ayers, University of Illinois

Challenges

A few challenges for you – which types of assessment would be appropriate for the following situations?

- To find out why a child in your group has tantrums.
- To find out if the role-play area is well used by both boys and girls.
- To find out if you should spend money on left-handed scissors.
- To find out where a particular child spends his/her time during child-initiated play.
- To find out whether a child in your group has a hearing problem.

So – you can choose! Of the methods described above, some will be familiar to you, others less so. The advantage of knowing what you *could* do, is that you have a whole range of assessment tools in your toolkit, and can make informed choices about how and when to use them – new ingredients for a new flavour of assessment.

Now on with recording!

5 From observation to records

This chapter is divided into two sections:

- Recording assessment for learning (AfL) – a continuous process, undertaken daily and weekly.
- Regular recording against agreed national or local standards – a periodic process, undertaken at intervals of about six to eight weeks.

Summing up this evidence and making judgements and writing down the things we find out, sifting out the important information, and recording it at regular intervals, is the next stage in our journey through assessment. Many settings and schools have agreed ways of recording ongoing assessments, and formats for recording children's achievements and developmental progress, others are still looking for the holy grail of the most time effective way of recording the huge amount of information we collect about each child. This chapter explores some of the different ways you could consider for recording your initial and ongoing observations of children's achievements and developmental progress.

Some of this information is part of the AfL processes, noting what you see as you see it. However, everyone needs to pause at regular intervals and look at what the information from AfL is telling us. These processes are collectively described as 'summative assessment' – summing up what we know so far, and recording the significant bits, often with some reference to national guidance, stages of development, or goals. The point at which 'formative assessment' (AfL) becomes 'summative assessment' is here – where assessment becomes recording.

What is the difference between formative and summative assessment in the early years?

Formative assessment is a process used by practitioners and teachers:	Summative assessment is a process used by practitioners and teachers:
• to **collect relevant evidence** of children's progress and achievements, mainly through observation of children in activities which they have initiated themselves • to **register and note significant achievements or difficulties**, not all of which are written down • to ensure that they observe and assess **every child** in their group or class • to provide immediate **feedback** on learning to children, their parents and to colleagues • to include and value **contributions from all the adults** in the setting, and in the child's family • to **inform planning** and next step, ensuring that future planning and target setting **improves teaching and learning** • to ensure that **observations are planned regularly**, and do not just happen randomly. *Formative assessment is often called 'Assessment for Learning' (AfL).*	• to **sum up information and assessments** at agreed intervals (usually at between six to eight weeks or half a term) • to take stock and **select key evidence** from AfL on which they can make judgements • to **assess progress against agreed outcomes or targets**, using common statements and indicators, usually from an agreed curriculum • to **condense information** by selecting significant pieces of evidence and incorporating these in manageable records • to **record** individual progress, on trackers, records or other documents • to **communicate information** to a range of audiences, including parents and the children themselves • to **ensure that the curriculum continues to meet the needs of the children**. *Summative assessment is often called record keeping or tracking.*

Formative assessment

Formative assessment almost always takes place in the setting when the children are present. It involves us in collecting evidence of various sorts, and it is important to remember that not all of this evidence will be written down.

Catching them at it!

'Evidence

Practitioners and EYFS profile moderators need to be aware that the definition of evidence is any material, knowledge of a child, anecdotal incident, result of observation or information from additional sources that supports the overall picture of the child's development. There is no requirement that evidence should always be formally recorded or documented.

Practitioners may choose to record specific evidence in order to secure their own judgements, but it is their final assessment of the child, based on all of their evidence (documented or not) that informs the completion of the EYFS profile, and it is this judgement that is moderated by the local authority. Most of the existing QCDA guidance refers to observing children in independent or self-initiated activities as a critical way in which evidence is collected and judgements made on what children really know and can do.'

Assessment and Recording Arrangements 2010 (ARA) (QCA, 2009)

Formative assessment in the early years is almost entirely done through observation, although small amounts of evidence can be usefully collected during adult-led sessions or by other assessment means. In England, the guidance on percentages suggests that 80 per cent of evidence should be collected during chid-initiated activities and a maximum of 20 per cent during adult-led or adult-initiated activities.

Summative assessment

Summative assessment involves us in sifting through all the evidence from formative assessment, including the evidence that has not been written down, and deciding what it is telling us about the child. Summative assessment almost always involves writing or recording our judgements, often on an agreed record, common across the setting, the school or even the local area. These are usually referred to as curriculum trackers or curriculum records.

'Practitioners should:
* make systematic observations and assessments of each child's achievements, interests and learning styles;
* use these observations and assessments to identify learning priorities and plan relevant and motivating learning experiences for each child;
* match their observations to the expectations of the early learning goals.'

Statutory Framework for the Early Years Foundation Stage (DCSF, 2008)

'Practitioners may choose to record specific evidence in order to secure their own judgements, but it is their final assessment of the child, based on all of their evidence (documented or not) that informs the completion of the EYFS profile.'

Assessment and Recording Arrangements 2010 (ARA) (QCDA, 2009)

The process of linking formative and summative assessment, and considering the evidence you have collected goes a bit like this:

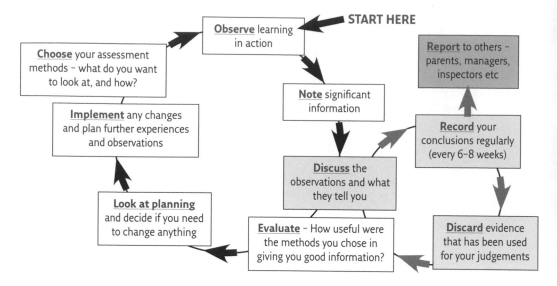

Making less from more – the art of condensing information

Whenever we decide to write something down, we inevitably condense it. Imagine writing down every single thing you see when you are observing a child, and imagine how long it would take to read! Even when we write a simple sticky note, or make a tick on a sheet, we are condensing our judgements of what we see and know about the child and writing the important bits.

At regular intervals we need to take all the 'already condensed' information in our AfL bag for each child and see what the collection is telling us. At this point we usually make an overall judgement, and record this on a schedule, tracker or profile, often using agreed statements to help with our decisions. In England, practitioners and teachers use the Development Matters statements and Early Learning Goals; in Wales and in Northern Ireland, the Pre-school Desirable Outcomes and the Key Skills statements in the Foundation Phase; and in Scotland, the Curriculum Areas in the Curriculum for Excellence and the agreed outcomes of this.

The chart on the following page attempts to describe how the English curriculum for the early years is condensed into a summative assessment of readiness for school, the EYFS Profile. At the end of the EYFS, 514 Development Matters statements are condensed into 115 Early Learning Goals, which are then condensed into 104 EYFS Profile statements plus 13 additional statements, which register attainment beyond the goals.

Catching them at it!

Condensing the curriculum through summative assessment

The curriculum areas	The components of the curriculum	Development Matters Statements in each component & how they are condensed		How the early learning goals appear in the 13 scales of the profile
Personal, social and emotional development				
100 development matters statements, concluding in 24 Early Learning Goals are condensed into 3 profile scales (24 statements)	Dispositions and attitudes Self confidence & self esteem Making relationships Behaviour and self control Self care Sense of community	22 22 17 11 16 12	100 Development Matters statements condensed to 24, plus 3 which recognise attainment beyond the goals	6 components condensed into 3 scales of 8 statements: *Dispositions and attitudes* *Emotional development* *Social development*
Communication, language and Literacy				
104 development matters statements, concluding in 20 Early Learning Goals are condensed into 4 profile scales (32 statements)	Language for communication Language for thinking Linking sounds and letters Reading Writing Handwriting	35 15 14 19 11 10	104 Development Matters statements condensed to 32, plus 4 which recognise attainment beyond the goals	6 components combined into four scales of 8 statements: *Language for communication & thinking* *Linking sounds and letters* *Reading* *Writing (including handwriting)*
Problem solving, reasoning and numeracy				
89 development matters statements, concluding in 47 Early Learning Goals are condensed into 3 profile scales (24 statements)	Numbers as labels and for counting Calculating Shape, space and measures	34 20 35	89 Development Matters statements condensed to 24, plus 3 which recognise attainment beyond the goals	Three scales of 8 statements *Number as labels & for counting* *Calculating* *Shape, space and measures*
Knowledge and understanding of the world				
82 development matters statements, concluding in 11 Early Learning Goals are condensed into 1 profile scale (8 statements)	Exploration & investigation Designing and making ICT Time Place Communities	18 12 10 16 9 17	82 Development Matters statements condensed to 8, plus 1 which recognises attainment beyond the goals	One scale of 8 statements for the whole of *Knowledge and Understanding of the world*
Physical development				
77 development matters statements, concluding in 8 Early Learning Goals are condensed into 1 profile scale (8 statements)	Movement and space Health & bodily awareness Physical development	37 16 24	77 Development Matters statements condensed to 8, plus 1 which recognises attainment beyond the goals	One scale of 8 statements for the whole of *Physical development*
Creative development				
62 development matters statements, concluding in 5 Early Learning Goals are condensed into 1 profile scale (8 statements)	Being creative Exploring media & materials Creating music and dance Developing imagination & imaginative play	15 19 16 12	62 Development Matters statements condensed to 8, plus 1 which recognises attainment beyond the goals	One scale of 8 statements for the whole of *Creative development*

The legal requirements for the assessment of the curriculum are clearly not the whole picture. If we are to capture the richness of each child's experience and each child's learning, we must do something more complex and use measures that are more sensitive than any summative assessment can provide.

Some of the ways in which AfL assessments can be recorded are now described. They are not in any particular order, except in going from the least formal and time consuming, to methods which need a real commitment of time and energy. They are followed by a selection of processes for summarising the information in summative assessments.

Some methods for recording AfL

Of course, we need to preface this section with a reminder that *not all observations are written down!* Some of the most useful information you collect about young children is collected almost unconsciously, like osmosis, soaking into your brain and memory through your eyes, ears and even your skin, enriching your knowledge of the child, and supporting your other judgements. However, we can't rely on this method alone. It is not systematic or reliable enough without planned observations and some note-making systems that ensure coverage of the curriculum and all the children.

Sticky notes or computer labels

This is a very common method, popular with practitioners. All the adults carry packs or sheets of these notes or labels with them as they work. They jot down informal observations of children's achievements as they work, collecting these as they go. Some settings and schools overprint sheets of computer labels with simple systems for circling areas of learning and so on as well as leaving space for information about individuals. Pads or sheets of these can also be left in a number of places around the setting/classroom and in outdoor areas for ease of use. Once completed, they are transferred to individual records or files. They are used in a similar way to notebooks.

Advantages
This method is good for jottings and odd notes. They can be easily transferred to individual files without re-writing. It is great for recording what parents say, and for using as you work.

Disadvantages
Some practitioners and teachers make this simple method into a chore by copying out all their notes again, rather than sticking the notes into children's records or onto index cards (see below). Sticky notes can prove expensive, but

computer labels (although more cumbersome) are cheaper. Another disadvantage is that notes can get lost. They are not useful for longer observations.

Index cards or postcards

These can be used to record children's individual developmental progress and achievements. Each child has a named index card, and these are used for informal jottings, logging other observations and making notes on activities such as paired reading. Some practitioners/teachers identify focus children for a day or a week by moving their cards to the front of the pile, and rotating these each week, so they focus on getting information about every child over half a term.

Advantages
This is a good, systematic way of ensuring that every child becomes the focus of your observations.

Disadvantages
This method should be used in conjunction with other methods such as observations, sticky notes and other ongoing records. If you *only* use this method, you may miss some important things because you are only looking at the focus child or children. In a big group it can take a long time to get through all the children if you only focus on one child at a time, hence the practice of identifying four or six focus children each week.

Notebooks or clipboards

Small notebooks are strategically placed in the setting or classroom both indoors and outside, where all practitioners have access to these notebooks as they work. They use the books to jot down their observations of significant achievements and/ or important events or incidents that may have occurred, naming individual children where appropriate.

Advantages
Notebooks are a great way for collecting jottings in an easily available format. They are accessible to all staff, and need little time to use.

Disadvantages
The notes need to be transferred to individual files or records, or vital information may be lost. This can be a time-consuming activity.

'Tick' sheets

Tick sheets, with children's names and spaces for a tick are often used for recording a simple skill achieved, an activity completed or a stage of development. Examples are 'Can recognise numbers from 1-5'; 'Can put on and fasten their own coat' or 'Has had a turn at cooking this half term'. These sheets are sometimes used over longer periods of time to record growing skills and aptitudes. In some settings, children are involved in completing the sheets which indicate involvement in particular activities such as cooking or ICT.

Advantages

Tick sheets are quick and simple to devise and complete. These sheets can help you to keep track of development and access to a range of activities or experiences, and several can be in use at the same time. Children can be involved in the recording.

Disadvantages

Tick sheets only record very simple information with little 'colour' to the judgement. Sometimes children can do a thing one day and not the next, or in one context and not another!

Observation sheets devised in the setting

Some settings agree on a format for recording observations. These often have pre-printed sections for recording names, dates, curriculum focus and so on. There are also spaces for recording the identified focus of the observation.

Advantages

These sheets are good for collecting systematic information, as you can make your own or personalise a blank for a specific activity or purpose.

Disadvantages

If you ONLY use these sheets, you could be missing things that are not on the list! They should be one of the tools, not the only one. A format for shorter observations and jottings should also be available.

Photographs

Digital and ordinary photographs are now routinely used to record children's achievements and progress. These are more useful if they are dated and annotated. Filing the photos in a digital folder for each child on the computer is one way of keeping track without having to print them all.

Advantages

This is an excellent way of capturing the moment, and children can get involved by taking photos of their own work and achievements, and recognising the efforts of others.

Catching them at it!

Disadvantages
Film development and colour printing can be expensive. If you take a lot of photos, sorting and annotating them can be time consuming. It's worth getting cameras that automatically date the photos.

Portfolios, learning journeys or records of achievement

Portfolios, more recently referred to as learning journeys are collections of children's work, photos, notes, observations and other information. Portfolios can include all the assessment information about one child, and they can be 'closed' (only accessible to adults and to parents on request), or 'open' (with the child fully involved in the collection and disposal of the contents).

Advantages
This method is very good for recognising the whole child and their progress across all aspects and interests. Most children love being involved. Information is all in one place for reporting to parents and getting an overview of the child. If they are 'rationalised' regularly by removing out of date or less useful contents, they can prove very informative at points of transfer.

Disadvantages
They can be time consuming to compile, particularly when children are involved. They also need to be weeded out regularly so the collection doesn't become too cumbersome. Everything should be dated, so a date stamp would be useful. Loose leaved versions can become very untidy!

Other technology

Video and audio tapes, and dictaphones can be used to record children's achievements and progress.

Advantages
These technologies are excellent for capturing the activities of children with additional needs, speech and language difficulties or mobility problems. They are also a useful tool for tracking progress over time in language, reading or social behaviour. Children enjoy using dictaphones to record their own activities.

Disadvantages
Audio tape recordings need to be transcribed if they are to be useful. These methods can be expensive in equipment and your time.

Methods of recording against national criteria: summative half-termly assessments

Paper-based tracking sheets - 'home grown'

Many schools and some early years settings have devised their own ways of keeping assessment records on paper. These follow the curriculum framework and practitioners tick, shade, highlight or otherwise indicate when statements, goals or levels are achieved. Some settings devise one simple sheet that covers all the goals or outcomes, and this is used alongside the curriculum guidance. This is very useful as an overview of the whole child across the whole curriculum.

Advantages
Tracking sheets on paper are more accessible for updating and interpretation than ICT based sheets, and this often makes it easier to involve others. The sheets are also easier to use when talking to parents or colleagues.

Disadvantages
Sometimes these trackers cover several sheets for each child, making them a bit cumbersome to use and interpret. Some settings devise complex 'keys' to indicate partial or less confident achievements – these are only useful if everyone understands what they mean!

Paper-based tracking sheets 'commercially' or locally produced

Some local authorities produce versions of these trackers for schools and settings to use, and others are available from publishers.

Advantages
Someone else has done the work, and as long as they fit your purpose, these can be great time-savers.

Disadvantages
Systems that have been devised outside your setting are often less successful than ones you have devised yourself, so you need to be sure you need an exterior model. In some cases practitioners do these external models, but also keep on with their own personal version, making double the work for themselves!

Condensed records of curriculum outcomes

Some local authorities, publishers and other suppliers, such as private nursery chains produce condensed versions of trackers for schools and settings to use. These provide overviews, some on a single sheet, with a key to indicate the relevant statements.

Advantages

Someone else has done the work, and as long as they fit your purpose, the single sheet versions could be very useful.

Disadvantages

The cost can be an issue, some may be more complex than you need, and if you need to see a reference document to complete and understand it, there could be a temptation to fill them in on 'autopilot'!

Computer-based (electronic) systems – 'home grown'

Many schools and some early years settings have devised their own ways of keeping digital assessment records. These vary from simple overviews of progress to complex e-portfolios containing photos, scans of children's work, practitioner notes and contributions from parents and the children themselves.

Advantages

These personalised e-portfolios can be a fantastic way of involving everyone in recording progress, recognising achievements over a period of time and including children's individual interests. If you have devised a system that works for you, you are more likely to put the time into making it work.

Disadvantages

These systems can be time consuming, even if children do some of it themselves. This method really appeals to practitioners who like ICT!

Computer-based (electronic) systems – commercially devised

Some computer-based systems are produced by commercial publishers and provider chains, and they allow practitioners and their managers to track progress against National Curriculum frameworks. Some also provide a range of ways of presenting information in charts and reports, which should enable practitioners to track children's development. Some also offer a tool to enable reporting to parents.

Advantages

There is quick retrieval of information in text and chart forms, particularly for evaluation and management purposes. Information can be produced in 'report to parents' format.

Disadvantages

This system needs dedicated time at regular intervals to transfer information from practitioner notes and so on. There is no space for photos. Reports to parents could seem a bit impersonal. Some systems need additional software, and cost may be an issue for some settings.

Methods of recording against national criteria: summative, end of stage assessments

Paper based systems – nationally devised

When the EYFS Profile was first produced, it was a paper version available to schools direct or to download from the internet. The paper version has now been superseded by the e-profile, a computer-based system, although it is still possible to submit the Profile outcomes on paper (Excel format available from www.teachernet.gov.uk/management/ims/datacollections/eyfsp/eyfspcollect10).

Advantages
Some smaller settings and schools prefer to use a paper version, so it is useful to have a version provided.

Disadvantages
Of course, when most schools and settings are using an electronic version, there may be some pressure to conform!

Computer-based (electronic) systems – nationally devised

As described above, the EYFS Profile in England is an 'end of stage' assessment, and its purpose is to summarise a huge amount of learning (over four or five years if you include pre-school and home experience) into a judgement on 'readiness' for the primary school curriculum. In England, this assessment condenses 514 Development Matters statements for the early years curriculum into 117 statements for assessment at the end of the early years curriculum. The Profile in England is also weighted towards personal, social and emotional development, communication and language development, and mathematics (Problem Solving, Reasoning and Numeracy) with a much lighter coverage of other areas (Knowledge and Understanding of the World, Physical Development, and Creative Development). These areas, where some children, and many boys excel, have much less weight in the final scores.

The e-profile is an example of a computer-based system designed by the government to assist the classroom practitioner in recording Profile assessments for the English curriculum. Other versions, including those used in the rest of the UK, are available to download from government departments, local authorities or to buy from publishers and other early years providers. They allow practitioners and their managers to track achievement of the Early Learning Goals, and provide a range of ways of presenting information in charts and reports. Many, including the e-Profile also offer a tool to enable reporting to parents. The e-profile can also be the method for sending attainment information to local and national government departments for use in comparisons.

Advantages

The profile provides a quick way of retrieving information across the whole curriculum for individual children, groups and cohorts. The information is often available in text and chart forms, particularly for evaluation and management purposes. Information can also be produced in 'report to parents' format. Comparisons across classes, groups, schools and local authorities are easy to see, and national averages are displayed alongside school and local results.

These profiles do provide useful information for the next teacher (usually the one who needs to find an entry point to the primary curriculum). They give a clear indication of whether the child is ready for the more formal learning that often follows early years experience.

Disadvantages

These computer-based profiles are highly condensed and are of little use for planning or observation. Their role is to summarise learning at the end of the year. They need dedicated time at regular intervals for the transfer of information from practitioner notes and so on. There is a danger that if the practitioner uses summative assessments too early in the final year of the early learning, their planning and observation may be restricted to the statements in the profile, not the wider bank of statements which represents the whole curriculum. This could be described as 'teaching to the test', and is likely to disadvantage some children whose achievements and interests fall outside the selected statements or the more heavily represented areas of learning.

Managing the evidence!

Once you have made your judgements and recorded them, you *don't* need to keep all the evidence! Some practitioners are worried about discarding evidence on which they have made their judgements, in case someone challenges them. However there is really no need to keep skip-loads of evidence 'just in case'. If you have made your judgements honestly and professionally, there is no need to keep every post-it note, every photo or every piece of work done by every child, and there is even less need to send all this on to the child's next teacher. The proper place for evidence that you no longer need is with the child, so send it home, unless the family already has a copy. Most children and their parents love to have their work.

A small collection of evidence can be useful to a new teacher or school and most teachers would say that between three and five pieces of work, well chosen by you, or by you and the child together, will be much more helpful to a new teacher than a big collection. These pieces of evidence of the child's interests and abilities should be dated and annotated if necessary.

Of course, selecting work for transfer is a time-consuming job, but if you plan time for it and do it with the children, it gives you a really good insight into what is important to the child, and how they want to be seen by their new teacher or practitioner. If you keep digital profiles with photos and other evidence in each child's folder on your computer, these can be put on disc for parents and for the next teacher or school. Digital profiles are a very cost effective way of keeping evidence, they take up very little space and can be accessed by the children.

Using assessment and records to help with planning next steps is a thread through this whole book. How we go about this delicate task is the focus for the next chapter.

6 What does planning for assessment look like?

Much of the guidance on assessment in the early years advises practitioners to 'use their observations to inform planning'. This is easy to say, but less easy to put into practice, so in this chapter I will be exploring how schools and settings can genuinely attempt this complex job. This is not the place for examples of planners or formats for planning which take into account the outcomes of assessment. The best planners are those that practitioners develop themselves, sometimes referring to guidance or the work of other settings, and regularly reviewing both the process of planning and the documentation used to record it. It is, however, possible to set out the *process* of planning for assessment, to offer some underlying principles for this, and to give examples of the process in action.

In the guidance for the Foundation Phase in Northern Ireland, there is a helpful description of the different layers of planning for the curriculum in the early years, and this will be familiar to most early years practitioners:

> 'Long-term plans set out, in broad terms, the learning for a whole group of children, usually over a period of a year.
>
> Medium-term plans bridge the gap between the broad outline of the long-term plan and the day-to-day detail of the short-term plan. Medium term plans may refer to half termly or monthly periods.
>
> Short-term plans should take account of the children's individual needs and be responsive to their ideas and spontaneous play. There should be enough detail to inform teachers and classroom assistants on a daily basis to ensure that the best use is being made of time, space and resources. These plans are likely to take account of recent observations and assessments of children.'
>
> *Understanding the Foundation Stage* (CCEA, 2006)

Most early years practitioners plan in this three-layered way, although their documentation may look different in its layout, content and quantity.

How do we make sure that there is time for assessment?

The only way to do this is to write it in your planning! It is vital to plan enough time for assessment at each of the layers of planning, because if we don't, this could happen:

'Without observation, overall planning would simply be based on what we felt was important, fun or interesting (or all three) but it might not necessarily meet the needs of the children in our care.'

Effective practice: Observation, Assessment and Planning
The Early Years Foundation Stage pack (CD-ROM) (DCSF, 2008)

In 'Ten tips for assessment' (see page 35) I suggest that 20 per cent of the time you spend with the children should be used for assessment. This rather scary amount of time will, of course, cover *all* the assessments you do when the children are there, including:

- observing children through planned and informal observations activities
- tracking children and activities
- taking photos and other recordings
- talking with children as they play and work, asking and answering questions
- collecting and organizing concrete evidence such as photos and copies of children's work
- listening to children as they talk, read, sing
- 'eavesdropping' and 'covertly watching' what children are doing, particularly in their play
- talking with parents about their children's achievements
- working with children to collect and select items for portfolios
- listening to children as they report back on their learning during group and plenary sessions
- explaining to children what you are finding out and writing about their learning.

There are, of course, other assessment activities that need to be planned into practitioners' work during the day, week and year. These include:

- contributing to informal discussions in the setting
- arranging and attending meetings to discuss planning and assessment
- attending training sessions
- getting involved in moderation of work in your setting and with practitioners from other settings
- sampling your evidence
- writing records and reports
- reporting to parents, managers and others
- analysing the results of your assessments.

If you start to count up the amount of time you spend on assessment, you will be amazed at how much you are doing, how often you are doing more than one of these things at a time, or how often you are making assessments as you do other

Catching them at it!

things! Of course, this collection of assessment techniques can't be allowed to just happen. Many of them take dedicated time, and there is never enough time when you are working in the early years. So planning for assessment needs to be consciously built in at every layer of planning. If you are unsure about any of the terminology used in this chapter, refer to page 55 for more information on assessment methods, and see the Ten tips for assessment on page 35.

Stop feeling guilty!

One of the most important things when planning for assessment is to stop feeling guilty! The fact that you are reading this book indicates that you know the vital role of assessment in and for learning, but some practitioners will still feel guilty when they think they are 'just watching children'. Some will also be less confident in writing observations, 'catching the moment' in photos, or asking open questions to get good information from children. These practitioners need support as they improve their confidence and their assessment techniques.

> 'Observation is the formal term for one of the most important aspects of day-to-day professional practice when working with children of all ages.'
>
> Effective practice: Observation Assessment and Planning
> *The Early Years Foundation Stage* CD-ROM (DCSF, 2008)

The managers and team leaders in every setting must make clear that planning time for observation, and using the resulting evidence are two of the most important tasks for settings. Managers must expect to see observation in action when they visit groups of children. They must include assessment practice in the range of targets for improvement for individuals and the setting as a whole. They must see training for assessment as a real reason for meetings and training sessions both on-site and further afield. And most importantly, they must expect to see time and staffing allocated to assessment activities in long, medium and short-term planning.

Planning should not just be an activity with its own life, going forward on a sort of 'autopilot', which could result in activities and opportunities that do not meet the needs of any of the children. What we all need to do is plan flexibly, be ready to change things as we begin to observe the planning in action, adjusting to what we see and what the children do. Of course, the first place that change will be needed is in short-term plans, the plans for the day and the week. These need to adjust to our daily observations, often to those we don't write down!

The best attitude to short-term planning is to plan in detail for the first day or two of the week, leaving the rest of the week in outline, and filling it up as the days develop, and children's needs emerge. This may mean some fairly dramatic adjustments and even abandoning something we have planned carefully on Sunday afternoon!

Planning needs to take into account the results of all your assessments, observations and other information. The different layers of planning will need to be adjusted in different ways, following different assessment methods, specifically chosen to give particular information.

What should short-term planning include?

Your short-term planning should be influenced by the notes and jottings you make in your daily work – sticky notes, notepads, photos, including the observations you don't even write down. It will be particularly responsive to what you see in child-initiated play activities, where the interests of individuals and small groups of children become evident; where you might pick up a lead for a new activity or centre of interest; identify the need for additional resources or see something that needs to be practised or reinforced. Adjusting your short-term planning is a daily possibility, as you ask yourself these questions:

● What have I seen today that may affect what I plan for tomorrow?
● Have any of the children asked for something that I could provide?
● Have I seen any emerging interests that I could promote tomorrow by planning activities, reading stories or introducing new resources?
● When I watch the children in independent activities, are they able to use the skills I am teaching them in adult-led sessions, or do I need to adjust the content of my group times?

To fulfill these professional expectations, your **short-term plans** might include time for some of the following assessment techniques:

● **Build assessment into your written planners** for the day and the week. How are you going to identify time and space for observation? Once you have identified the time when the planned observations will happen, how will everyone know who you are going to look at and what you are looking for?

● **Make sure there is always at least one person concentrating on observation during child-initiated sessions.** This time will involve you in participant observations, don't try to do group work during these sessions!

'Participant observations are observations you note down while you are fully involved with the children, noting down significant things you see. Although this might be most of what you observe, it is important that some observations are planned, so that time is set aside for you to watch the children at play.'

Effective practice: Observation Assessment and Planning
The Early Years Foundation Stage CD-ROM (DCSF, 2008)

Catching them at it!

- Provide **plenty of jotters, sticky notes, stickers and simple observation sheets** around the setting, indoors and outside, so you can jot down significant information. Set up a simple way of organising these jottings so they are easily managed and accessible for discussions.

- **Leave time at the end of each adult-led session to quickly record the significant things that happened** – were all the children engaged? Did any child find this activity too difficult or too easy? Did any child surprise me, amaze me, worry me or puzzle me? This can be done on a simple sheet with the children's names listed. Remember, don't write about everything, just jot down the significant things.

- **Use cameras** to capture the moment. Digital cameras give you instant access to the things you see, so you can look at today's photos on the camera or a computer during your planned discussions.

- Plan to have **two adults present some of the time at group times**, one leading the session, the other observing all the children, or children who are the current focus.

- **Use Key Person groupings** as the organisation for small group times, so the person who knows these children best is able to observe their own group.

- **Set up a system for identifying 'focus children'**. This could be a file card index or other simple system to ensure you cover and revisit all the children regularly.

- **Plan some time for longer observations** when you can look at individual children more closely. Remember the guidance, and don't make these observations too long. It's better to plan more short observations than long ones that just put pressure on everyone:

'These planned observations usually last for anything from between three and ten minutes. Very occasionally they may be longer if resources allow.'

Effective Practice: Observation, Assessment and Development
The Early Years Foundation Stage CD-ROM (DCSF, 2008)

- Discuss whether you could **build in some simple tracking** of activities or individuals to make sure you know what is happening in different activities or areas of the room or outdoor area.

- Make some sheets of **tips for assessing play** in different areas of your provision, listing some of the things you are looking for. Put these up in the areas of provision and the tips will remind you of what you are looking for in child-initiated play.

- **Make time at the end of the session or the day** to look at your observations and share them in the team. Have your short-term plan available too, so you can make adjustments on the spot.

- **If you are worried about an individual child**, plan some observations over a week, so you can collect information from different observers and in different activities. Remember:

  'There is no requirement that evidence should always be formally recorded or documented.'

  Assessment and Recording Arrangements 2010 (ARA) (QCA, 2009)

What should medium-term planning include?

Your medium-term planning should be influenced by your regular record keeping. Every six to eight weeks, when you review your latest units of work, topics and skills development, recording the outcomes on children's curriculum records, you will reflect on whether your medium-term plans are meeting the needs of all the children. You will be using the children's curriculum records to track progress towards the targets and goals you have set, and using the process to think about the curriculum for individuals and groups within your class. Adjusting your medium-term planning is a possibility every half term, by asking questions such as:

- Are we going too fast or too slowly through the curriculum?
- Are we managing to provide that ideal balance of security and challenge that really does scaffold children's learning?
- Are we meeting the needs of this particular group?
- Are any children getting left behind?
- Do any children need more challenge?
- Is the balance of child-initiated and adult-led activity about right for the children?

Your **medium-term planning** should include time for some of the following assessment techniques:

- **Plan some meeting and discussion time to look at:**
  - **The records of individual children and groups** to see if there are any patterns across different records.
  - **Coverage** – did you actually cover everything you planned?
  - Your planning and record keeping **process**, is it manageable and useful? Does it help you to manage the week and the half term?

    'The task of keeping records must be manageable and sustainable. Practitioners should be realistic about the amount of information they collect and the systems

they create. These need to be manageable as part of day-to-day practice.' *Creating the Picture* (DFES, 2007)
  – The guidance to see how well you are **covering the curriculum**.
  – A sample of children's **portfolios** to see if you have the right amount and range of assessment evidence.
  – The previous half term's **topic** or centre of interest. Did it go well? Were the children interested? What did they learn?

● In the plan for the next half term, build in:
  – Some **tracking** of activities and use of areas.
  – **Time to talk with the children** about what they know, can do and are interested in.
  – Time to **go through portfolios** to make sure they are manageable and well organised.
    'The activity of record-keeping must be selective so that it remains manageable and to ensure that important information is not obscured. This selection will depend on practitioners having a good understanding of children's development and learning.' *Creating the Picture* (DFES, 2007)
  – Any **adjustments to the planning and recording process** that you have decided to make.

What should long-term planning include?

Your long-term planning should be influenced by your annual review of the curriculum, looking at how you manage the development of learning through a mixture of methods – the range of themes and topics; continuous and enhanced provision for child-initiated learning; the condition, use and access to resources and the way you help children to make progress in skills development. You will be using end-of-year assessments, such as annual reports, transfer records, and formal assessments, such as the EYFS Profile in Reception. Adjusting your long-term planning is a possibility every year. You will consider this at the end of the year as you reflect on the past year and the current group of children and ask:

● Were the children engaged with the topics and themes we introduced, or should we consider revising the topic cycle to incorporate more of the children's own interests?
● Do our records and reports reveal any gaps in children's learning?
● Did we miss anything vital?
● Did the children develop in the way we expected?
● Is there any way we can adjust next year's planning so it is more effective?
● Do we need any additional resources, or have we got resources that we are not using?

At the beginning of the new academic year, you will also look at your new group or class and consider whether your long-term plan is likely to meet the needs of the new group, as no two classes or groups of children are the same. Some questions might be:

- What is the gender balance of this group?
- Is this a young class, with the majority of children born in the spring and summer months?
- Will the cultural or ethnic balance of this group indicate different interests, language levels, social development?
- Are the children coming into my group straight from home, and what will this mean for my planning?
- How will our evaluation of last year affect next year?

Your **long-term planning** should include time during, and particularly at the end of the year for some of the following activities:

- **Plan some meeting and discussion time to look at and discuss:**
  - any **data** resulting from end-of-year records and assessments to locate any trends and gaps
  - information about the year and the group, resulting from writing **annual reports and records** and discussing these with parents and children
  - **your annual (long-term) plan** for the curriculum
  - your **cycle of topics, centres of interest** or themes
  - any information about **resources** you need to add, replace, reorganise or repair.

- In the plan for the next year, build in:
  - further **tracking** of activities and use of resources
  - time for **discussion** of assessment in informal sessions and more formal meetings
  - any **modifications you want to make to the planning and assessment** process at all three levels
  - any decisions you have made on **curriculum coverage, organisation and balance** of activities, such as your topic cycle or session plans
  - a point at the end of the year when you will discuss how well the year has gone.

And to conclude this section, here are some examples from practice:

- **Four practitioners** are tracking the way children access resources and are able to take them to the area of the setting that they choose. This gives them information about the organisation and layout of the resources, and will affect planning for the whole setting at long-term level.

- **Information from the EYFS Profile** is analysed by Maura and her teaching assistant. They find that the children in the current group, particularly the boys, have low scores in fine motor control and using small tools. They look at their medium-term plan and how they could improve opportunities and resources for more fine motor activities, particularly during child choice times and in the outdoor area. They add some smaller tools and equipment to water play, mark making and the 'making area'. They also teach children how to use the tools in adult-led activities. During the rest of the year they monitor the use of these tools and add more as the boys become better at using them. The increased opportunity to use tools improves the skills of all the children in the group.

- **Danny observes a group of girls** in the role-play area. They are trying to make some clothes for a baby doll. They are using paper and are disappointed in their own efforts when the paper clothes fall off the baby. Danny offers some easy-to-cut fabric and fabric glue to make the job easier. The girls get very involved in this activity, but their scissor skills are not very good, and they need a lot of help. Danny adjusts his short-term plan again to plan some small group activities with scissors to improve the scissor skills of all the children.

- **The teachers in Reception** plan a topic about the seaside as part of their long-term topic cycle. They prepare a medium-term plan and then talk with the children about what they already know about the seaside. During this session they find that the majority of the children have never been to the seaside. The teachers postpone the topic until they find out whether they could take the children to the seaside before they embark on this part of their long-term plan.

- **At the end of the afternoon, two boys find a blue shopping bag** at the bottom of the brick box. They start to play a simple shopping game and are very disappointed when packing-up time is announced. The teaching assistant in the group observes this play, and adjusts her plan for the next day to include setting up a small role-play shop where she leaves the blue shopping basket. The following day she finds the two boys and tells them what she has provided. One of the boys is very excited and immediately gets involved in the shop play, where two other children join him.

- **Jodie and Mina are discussing the records of their key groups** of children. They note that there is no information for some children on whether they can 'sing simple songs from memory' – one of the Early Learning Goals for creative development. They plan to make this a focus for observation. They provide some nursery rhyme tapes and books for the book corner, and include more singing in group times, offering children the opportunity to perform a song to the group if they want to. Many do, and love doing it. Jodie and Mina get lots of information about singing, they find out that children are singing everywhere

– outside, on the bikes, in doll play in the home corner, in the book corner – as well as during small group times.

- **Sammy is one of the focus children** for observation in his pre-school group. During the week, the adults notice his interest in books, and particularly non-fiction books about animals. They plan a visit to the library for the following week, inviting parents to come too. Sammy's mum joins the library with Sammy and the librarian offers to come to the pre-school to read stories once a week. To Sammy's delight she asks him if he would like her to bring some animal stories. The adults decide to include regular visits to the library in their medium-term plans.

- **Bernice is a childminder** who looks after her own small baby and Sandy (aged three and an only child). When they visit the local child-minding group Bernice notices that Sandy stays very close to her and will not join the other children in their play, becoming distressed when Bernice encourages her to join in. Bernice talks to Sandy's parents and they decide that Sandy needs more opportunities to meet and play with other children, before she starts school. Bernice contacts another childminder and arranges to share activities with her on a regular basis, planning joint visits and meeting in each other's homes. By the time Sandy goes to school, at four, she is much more comfortable playing with other children, although she still sometimes needs support.

These examples give some idea of the many ways that practitioners adjust their planning in response to what they observe, asking questions and examining their practice.

Of course, reviewing and asking questions often results in change to planning. However, we should remember that asking the questions does not always result in dramatic change. The answers sometimes give us positive reinforcement that we are in fact doing the right thing, and that the planning really is meeting the children's needs. In this case, no change is needed.

> 'The key issue is that you should observe children on a regular basis, at different times of the day, and all staff should be involved. Decisions about a child's needs should not be based on just one observation. This means ensuring that each child is observed systematically, over time, by staff and that regular discussions take place to consider what has been learned to help you plan for the child's development and learning.'
>
> Effective Practice: Observation, Assessment and Development
> *The Early Years Foundation Stage* CD-ROM (DCSF, 2008)

Catching them at it!

7 Feedback to parents – your child, your future

'Parents know their children intimately. For practitioners, therefore, building a close, trusting and reciprocal relationship with parents needs to begin before a child starts in a setting. Parents need to be involved as part of the ongoing assessment process, sharing their views and observations about the child's development with practitioners and being involved in planning what opportunities and experiences to offer the child next.

Where appropriate, bilingual support services should be employed to ensure effective two-way communication between parents and the setting as well as to support children's learning.'

Effective practice: Observation, Assessment and Planning
The Early Years Foundation Stage CD-ROM, (DCSF, 2008)

If we return to the triangular diagram presented earlier in the book, you will see that reporting features at the top of the triangle, where information is at its most condensed, where there is sometimes limited time or opportunity for feedback, and when the process can seem at its 'coldest' and most automatic. Of course this function of assessment (summative, annual meetings with parents and carers) does not represent the richness of contact with a child's parents during the early years, when the family is in closest touch with the setting and the adults who work there.

Reporting

Recording

Assessment for learning
(formative and summative)

Giving feedback through reporting to parents and others is one of the most important aspects of assessment, because if we want the outcomes of our observations to be effective in improving learning and progress, everyone needs to know what is happening. Of course, it is much easier and more effective if the information, particularly at points of transition, is condensed and presented in a form that parents can understand.

However, this book is not just about summative assessment, its major focus is AfL, a process which is continuous throughout the year. If parents understand how this works, they can feel confident that they are helping their children in the best possible way. The following quote from *Creating the Picture* gives some idea of the complex task this is for practitioners, another responsibility in a very busy job, but a vital cornerstone for children.

> '**Assessments must actively engage parents in developing an accurate picture of the child's development.** Effective partnership, working with parents, will ensure that their vital perspective contributes to the overall description of children's development and learning.
>
> What it looks like
>
> This principle is demonstrated when practitioners adopt these strategies:
>
> - Acknowledge parents to be the prime and first educators of children.
> - Engage in a two-way flow of information between family and setting, in order to meet children's needs effectively and agree next steps in learning.
> - Support parents in describing their children's individual attainment.
> - Talk with parents and involve them in reviews of their children's achievements, including those demonstrated at home.'
>
> *Creating the picture* (DFES, 2007)

Ten tips for involving parents in AfL

Children who know that the key people in their home and their Key Person in the setting are working together in their interests, will feel more secure, and will therefore learn better. So how do we make that process work, how do we make it manageable in a busy setting, with parents who are busy too? What are the key factors that work for good communication and inclusive practice in AfL in the early years? These **Ten tips for involving parents in AfL** may help, and they are all things you can easily build into regular practice in your setting:

1. **Recognise the parents' role as first educator, and start early** – make sure that parents' voices are heard before the child is admitted to your setting. Visit them at home if you can, and explain what AfL looks like, bring some photos and include some of children talking with other adults or other children about their work and parents spending time looking at folders or portfolios with their children. Find out what the child likes, dislikes, their interests and concerns. Make sure that the pre-admission visit is a positive experience, that you listen more than you talk, and that parents don't feel bombarded by questions that seem like a test! Make some notes and check them with the parents before you leave, so they know what you have written. This builds the sort of trust you need for real partnership.

   An example: *Pat and Sue, early years practitioners, visit a family together. One takes some toys, so they can play with Sam (the child), the other talks with the parents and makes some notes. They have some prompts for their conversation, but these are not just questions, more invitations to tell them about the child. They take photobooks of the setting in action, and an invitation to come for some pre-admission visits as a family. Before they leave, Pat (who will be Sam's Key Person) asks if she may take a picture of the family together, explains a bit about her role and checks the notes with the parents before she leaves.*

2. **Make sure you use this early information** – it's no use if you just put it in a cupboard, so incorporate it in your planning for welcoming the child on the first steps in your setting. Make sure you have the sorts of things in your setting that will make the child feel secure. Spend time with them during the first days and weeks, as they show you what they can do. Feed back to parents on any inconsistencies in behaviour or any worries that you may have, but make sure these are presented positively!

   An example: *As Pat and Sue drive back to the setting, they talk about the family and how they can help Sam to settle. They note that he seems a rather lacking in confidence and may take longer to settle than some of the other children.*

They also note his interest in the photobook, and particularly the train track. This will be the first piece of information Pat puts in his Interest Tracker (a simple sheet in his portfolio that records his developing interests).

3. **Include parents at every stage of the process** – if parents really feel they know you, and you are making a real effort for their child, they are almost certain to be more open to giving and getting information about their child. Remember that children only start school once, it's important to get it right, as we can't go back and do it again! First impressions are lasting ones for children and their parents.

An example: This setting has a policy of staggered entry and pre-admission visits are spread over the last half term before the child enters. The children come in twos and threes, and visit while the previous group of children are still in the class. This seems to help in many ways.

On Sam's pre-admission visit, there is a 'Welcome to Sam' poster on the door of the setting, with the photo of him with his family. The train set is out and some other boys welcome him by including him in their game. His mum and dad have both made the effort to come for this visit, and Pat makes sure she has time to talk to them, as she shows them round the setting, explaining what is going on. One of the older children is asked to show them her folder where she keeps originals, copies and photos of her learning, each one dated and some with comments written by the practitioners. There are also some comments from the girl's parents.

Before they leave, Pat gives the parents a card with her name and the contact numbers of the setting. On the back of the card are some simple tips for helping children to settle when they first start:

> **What you can do to help your child to settle in:**
> Read a story to them every day.
> Make sure they have enough sleep.
> Give them time to eat some breakfast, even if you don't!
> Tell them you love them every day.
> Tell us if you are going to be late at home time.

4. **Make your setting accessible** – go outside regularly and look at your front entrance with a parent's eyes. Does it look and feel welcoming? Do you have children's work or photos on display? Have you got helpful signs so they know where to go? Is there somewhere comfortable and welcoming to wait? Is there helpful information on parenting and the curriculum for parents on a noticeboard or table, and copies for them to take home?

Catching them at it!

An example: *The entrance to this setting is very small, it is near a busy road. Obviously the staff must make sure the children are secure, but the practitioners have made the small area welcoming with flowers, a small settee, a basket of baby toys and a small noticeboard for information. There are also some photos of the setting in action. On the doors through to the three group rooms are photos of the children and adults who work there. On the outside of the door is a welcome notice in several languages.*

5. **Give plenty of informal opportunities for parents to contribute information** – do parents genuinely feel welcome? Is there really an open door through which they can come, or do they get the message that you are very busy and they can only see you if they are very 'pushy' or have an emergency? Some parents find it very difficult to come into settings and although they may have some valuable information, they need encouragement to stay and talk.

An example: *Pat, Sue and their colleagues have worked hard to make the setting a place where parents can come at any time. They schedule their day so the children and their parents begin each session with child-initiated activities, which means the staff are available to listen to parents and to give them some informal feedback about how things are going. They can also explain what is happening when children play, by observing what is going on in the room.*

Photos of the setting at different times of the day are displayed, so parents see other activities where children are learning in groups, going to different parts of the building, meeting other adults or making new friends. There are also packs of sticky notes for parents to jot down significant information about home. Any important information about individual children, which everyone should share (such as new babies, holidays and so on), is written on a 'Breaking news' board, and the practitioners make a note of anything which is more confidential or sensitive.

6. **Include everyone** – some parents find it difficult to spend time in your setting because they are working, others are less confident, some have such stressful lives that they just can't face any more responsibility, and a very few remain stubbornly unavailable.

An example: *In Pat and Sue's setting, they make every effort to make sure every parent has equal access to information. They know the staff can't make parents use this, and there are some who don't. In addition to their availability at the start of each session, they encourage parents to choose the methods they find easiest. One parent, who is disabled, has weekly contact by phone to provide information about her child's progress; another uses the Internet to email information – she knows she may not get a detailed reply, but it makes her feel much more involved. Some parents like diaries for messages from home – they*

know that the practitioners may not have time to reply every day, but they will always read and initial each entry, commenting if they feel the need. Others (particularly those whose children attend after-school care) ask for the children's profiles or some photos to keep them up to date (it is heartening to note that none of these vital collections has ever been lost!).

7. **Meet regularly to discuss the child** – this is helpful, both in understanding the child and in building trust with parents. This *doesn't* mean frequent *formal* meetings, but making the most of the points in the day when parents are most likely to be around, and adding to these by offering other opportunities for parents to be involved in the life of the setting. For many parents, these opportunities will provide less threatening times and places for discussing their child. Of course, you have to report formally every so often to discuss how their child is progressing against the curriculum objectives, but this conversation becomes a continuation of the relationship they are building with you, not a confrontation with the possibility of blame and guilt on their part.

   An example: *In Pat and Sue's setting the staff try to expand the opportunities for informal contact each year, and next year they are going to try offering an email service to working parents. This will build on the current 'incoming message system' by adding a feature where the children and staff can send emails to their parents, which, to begin with, will only be for photos of pieces of work or activities that will be included in the child's portfolio. If this works, they may expand it in the future but if it proves to be unmanageable, they may discontinue it.*

   Existing opportunities to become involved include helping during sessions; accompanying the group on walks and visits; free access to their child's portfolio at the beginning and end of the day and an appointment system for longer discussions, particularly when parents are worried. They also meet the parents with their child every term to look together at the portfolio, and talk about next steps.

8. **Explain what you are doing** – if parents are to understand what you are trying to do in supporting AfL, they need you to explain and demonstrate what it is. Most parents will only have experienced more formal sorts of assessment, with marks and grades, with little explanation of how they could make their work better. If you do some specific things to support learning to learn, explain them to parents in photos, short notes home, newsletters and in meetings.

   An example: *When Pat and Sue started to use AfL techniques, they had a workshop before they started to explain their plans to parents. This involved explaining what sharing learning intentions with children, and 'two stars and a*

wish' involved (see page 104). Parents who couldn't attend the workshop could see what happened in photos displayed on the parents' noticeboard, and could take an explanatory sheet to read at home. The members of staff in the setting encourage parents to ask when they don't understand what is going on, as children do sometimes come home with a mixed description of what is happening!

9. **Get the children to help** – the children will be enthusiastic about involving their parents. They love seeing their parents in their setting, and will welcome any opportunities to do this. Be imaginative – some parents find it difficult to come during the day and this may make their children feel left out. How are you going to make opportunities for these parents to join their children? Remember that social events can make a big difference to working parents and those who are less confident, as they aren't too 'teachery'!

   An example: Pat, Sue and their colleagues have always welcomed parents into the setting, and they are always looking for new ways, of which the email system described earlier is one. Children are also encouraged to invite their parents to see what they have been doing during the day. They take photos home in their book bags, and they bring objects, photos and other significant objects to the setting, including an increasing range of the foods they eat and the clothes they wear at home, for festivals and special occasions. A small group of parents (including one dad) come in to cook with the children, widening the children's experiences of food from around the world.

   During last year they had a real push on involving dads, by helping the children to organise some Saturday gardening and DIY sessions to improve the outdoor environment – planting a sensory garden and building a new pond. The children wrote invitations and made posters, they also helped with the snacks, and really enjoyed helping their parents in the setting. Everyone loved these events and they were well supported, particularly the one with a barbecue at lunchtime, and more events are planned.

   Many of these events are about enhancing experiences for children, but the great spin-off is a real community approach to education.

10. **Don't be too ambitious – start small!** the setting described in the examples is very well established. The members of staff have worked in the setting for many years and know the area and the parents well. They have developed their work with parents over many years. Starting small is essential, decide on one thing you want to try next year, and don't expect one thing to suit all parents. Look carefully at the children and their families and decide on a suitable strategy that fits your unique setting and the unique families it supports. Ask a few parents how they would like to be more involved in and informed about your work and how they can give you more information about their children. Try some of their

ideas, and don't forget the children. Watch them, welcome their parents in and just get talking – this is often the very best way of getting going.

An example: When Pat and Sue started their work with parents, they thought they knew what the parents wanted. They drew up a rota for parent helpers and asked the parents to sign up for a regular slot. The parents in their area hated the idea! They were not well organised enough to reserve a consistent commitment, and they were worried about what they would be asked to do. No-one signed up! Pat and Sue went back to the drawing board and considered some other ways that did not put so much pressure on the parents.

Parents have so much to offer us as we work with their children, but it is sometimes difficult to get the right balance between parental involvement and too much pressure on children, practitioners and parents themselves. However, in settings where parents feel really valued as their child's first and enduring teacher, the practitioners feel trusted and confident, children are happier, and happy children certainly learn more.

The next and final chapter in this book places the children firmly in focus as we conclude our journey through assessment for learning.

8 Involving the children – two stars and a wish for the future

Although this is the final chapter, it is far from just a conclusion! What you do with the information you collect from assessment, not merely to plan and track the curriculum, or compile annual reports to parents, but to change things for children, is one of the most important roles for you as a practitioner.

AfL in the early years

The previous chapter addressed how you could use AfL to inform your planning for future learning. This chapter is about using the same information to help children and their families to understand what they are learning now and how to improve learning in the future.

Of course, older children can be helped to do this by displaying posters, written comments, helpful marking, talk partners, traffic lights, 'no hands up' and all the other well-publicised AfL techniques that encourage children to think about learning.

In the early years it is both more difficult and more important to harness the power of feedback. Very young children live for the moment and need immediate feedback, and they respond more to pictures than words, and more to people than to paper, however brightly coloured the poster might be! They need their feedback to be tailored to their current interests and to be worded in ways that support their confidence and competence as young learners. If we give them too much information, or messages that are too complex, we risk undermining their self-image and self-esteem. Instead of becoming more competent and confident, some may shut down and become passive, over-reliant on adults, or even worse, aggressively defensive.

However, the majority of young children are smart and resilient! They know when we are being honest with them, and they have a very good idea of how much effort they have been making. They may need some help in identifying what 'good' means in any given situation, but once they do, they can become very reflective about their own and others' learning:

> 'Put at its simplest, AfL focuses on pupils knowing what 'good' looks like in any given learning context.'
>
> *Assessment for Learning: A Practical Guide* (CCEA, 2009)

To be successful, feedback for young children should always be:

- honest
- specific to the child, their interests and abilities
- positively worded
- balanced
- relevant to them
- timely, and close to the action
- focused on the learning, not on the child
- frequent, but not constant.

Feedback can backfire or become counter-productive, particularly for very young children, if it is:

- **too kind** – 'What a clever girl, you **have** worked hard!'
- **too vague** – 'That's lovely!'
- **too critical** – 'That's wrong!'
- **too excessive** – 'What a wonderful painting you have done, you're a real artist!'
- **too late** – 'I just want to say that I think you were a really kind friend when we went to the park last week'.

Examples added to quote from *Assessment for Learning: A Practical Guide* (CCEA, 2009).

Keeping the balance of positive reinforcement and honest support for improvement is important, and the techniques for using AfL need practice, particularly when working with very young children, where we sometimes have less room for manoeuvre or time for reflection. Fortunately, the people who are constructing today's early years guidance have taken note of research, and are incorporating key elements into the curriculum that are not only helpful to brain development and delivery of the curriculum, but in AfL.

In the UK, the Northern Ireland Council for Curriculum, Examinations and Assessment (CCEA) has been at the forefront of embedding AfL in the National Curriculum, making it more than a way of simply monitoring progress, but the key way to improve learning. This work has resulted in *Assessment for Learning: A Practical Guide*, which gives guidance to teachers in Northern Ireland, and has been a significant influence on the latest version of the curriculum for the early years (The Foundation Stage), where guidance helpfully describes AfL in the early years in these ways:

'Effective questioning is also an integral part of observation and assessment practice in the Foundation Stage.
Adults should use questioning to:
- clarify or extend children's thinking;
- interact sensitively with children to support their learning on topics of mutual interest;

- engage children in reflective discussion about their learning;
- make judgements on what children understand and can do;
- model the effective use of questioning.

Feedback in the Foundation stage should primarily be oral and should take place throughout the learning process. When giving feedback to children, adults should remember:
- young children need a nurturing climate;
- verbal and non-verbal language from the adult gives powerful messages to the child about his/her ability;
- to focus feedback on individual progress;
- to give feedback that focuses on success and improvement; and
- to give children time to make improvements.'

Understanding the Foundation Stage,(CCEA, 2006).

The learning environment

For such guidance to be effective practitioners should be aware of the impact of the learning environment on young children, and here *Assessment for Learning: A Practical Guide* can help us. The three essentials are **structure, skills and information**. After each of the these (below), I have explored what each one means for early years practitioners trying to establish AfL for children under five:

'Structure: Classrooms with significant levels of independent learning tend to be much more structured. They have clear procedures for everything, from accessing and returning resources and pursuing learning activities, to using the teacher's feedback to make improvements in learning.'

High quality curriculum guidance for the early years across the world promotes independent learning, supporting practitioners in providing child-led activities in an 'safe, secure, yet challenging environment' *Practice Guidance for the Early Years Foundation Stage (DCSF, 2008)*. Independent learning can only flourish in an environment where some things are predictable, and there is an order and permanence to the day, to objects and to relationships.

'Skills: Invest time in helping pupils to develop their independent learning skills. Teach them how to ask and answer questions, how to use success criteria to negotiate learning activities and use feedback effectively, and how to manage the demanding skills of reflecting about their own (and others') learning.'

Early years settings are places where children have the opportunity to both learn and practise key skills. An essential part of developing skills is to have good models! Young children need time to develop skills, they need to see adults and older children modeling learning and personal skills in ways that inspire young learners to learn them too. Being an independent thinker, a good questioner and a reflective practitioner are essentials for those working in the early years.

'Information: Provide sets of information in child-friendly language that enable pupils to access support during their learning activities. This information may be in the form of success criteria or reminders of strategies and procedures, such as questioning and feedback. These play an important role in reducing the pressure on pupils' memory to hold such information. This can often make the difference between independence and over-reliance on you or their peers.'

Of course, most of the children in the early years are just beginning to become readers and writers, so 'child-friendly language' will need to be mainly spoken, with pictorial clues to help young memories. Pictures, words and simple language will be most effective in the early years setting, but this does not mean patronising children or lowering our expectations. As most of us know, children are much smarter than we might think, and can take much more control of their own learning than we sometimes allow.

Once they are able to read simple text, these expectations could be presented in the following format:

Learning intention	Success criteria
We are learning to help at clearing up time.	<ul><li>Remember where things are kept.</li><li>Help with everything, not just the things you have been playing with.</li><li>Everyone helps.</li></ul>
We are learning to listen to each other.	<ul><li>Look at the person who is speaking.</li><li>Don't do anything else while they are speaking.</li><li>Think about what they are saying.</li></ul>

In early years settings, the setting and evaluating of group expectations is likely to be a weekly occurrence, with intentions frequently focusing on big learning issues, such as 'working together' and 'good listening'.

Catching them at it!

AfL in the early years checklist

If we construct an 'AfL in the early years checklist', what will it contain, and what are the challenges it will present to us?

1. **Independent learning - settings where independent learning is embedded appear to offer children a magical balance of freedom, clear structures for learning, and safe risk, which results in better learning.**

   What does independent learning look like in our setting? Is it true independence (autonomy) or are children just engaged in 'hands on, brains off' play activities with no structure and no support from us, while we do something else? Are children able to take 'safe risks', both in the environment and in their learning? Do we subtly make choices for children by 'putting things out' for them, or suggesting that some activities are more important to us than others?

2. **Clear learning intentions - settings where practitioners share clear learning intentions with children are more likely to be able to implement AfL. If children are clear about what we expect them to learn, they are much more likely to be able to concentrate on the activity and talk about whether they are successful or not.**

   Do we present independent learning in a framework of clear expectations? How do children know what we want them to learn? How do we share learning intentions with them? How often do we discuss these when the activity is over?

3. **A focus on children as individuals - settings where practitioners know about individuals and their families, observing children to find out their current interests and any difficulties, will be able to support AfL. The Key Person approach supports AfL. If children understand that adults know them as individuals, appreciate their strengths, interests, worries and fears, they will be more confident as they learn how to learn and evaluate their own learning.**

   Do we really know each child as an individual? How do children know that we are interested in them as individuals? How do we include their families, cultures and interests as we plan new experiences?

4. **Sensitive questioning - settings where practitioners are good at asking open questions that really make children think will be nurturing AfL. These practitioners will also be good at encouraging children to ask questions as well as answering them!**

   Do we know how to ask open questions? Do children have opportunities to ask questions too? How much time do we give to sustained shared thinking where adults and children spend time thinking together?
   'Use open questions and give thinking time - 5 seconds will really give them time to think.' *Assessment for Learning: A practical Guide* (CCEA, 2009)

5. <u>Prompts and reminders of our expectations</u> – settings where practitioners help children to get it right by reminding them appropriately about what is expected of them, and by modelling thinking, questioning, trying things out, even making mistakes, so children know that is the way to become a good learner.

Are we clear about what we expect? Do we remind children, before and during activities of what we are expecting (our criteria for success)? Are we good models for the children in our care – do we practice what we preach? Do we make our expectations for the whole group explicit, and do we praise children when they reach them?

6. <u>Keeping feedback positive</u> – settings where positive feedback outnumbers suggestions for improvement, and negative feedback is phrased in positive terms, are more likely to be successful. There is evidence that the ratio of two to one, two positives to each point for improvement is the best balance for maintaining a positive environment and relationships. This is sometimes referred to as 'two stars and a wish', where children are more likely to be able to focus on improvement, while still feeling successful.

Do we keep this ideal balance when giving feedback to children? Do children get two stars and a wish from us, and are they clear about which is which? Do we model this when we feed back to each other as practitioners?

7. <u>A focus on clear feedback and next steps</u> – children in settings where they have clear feedback will be more confident and more likely to become better learners. If they also have some idea of where to go next (the ways they could improve).

Is our feedback to children really clear, and focused on the learning intentions and criteria for success? Do we really help children to understand what they can do to improve, and is this clearly linked to the learning intentions we have shared with them?

8. <u>Making it manageable</u> – managing this process is time consuming and can result in pressure for practitioners and children. Deep concentrated feedback is not possible for every child in every activity every day. The ideal times are during child-initiated learning, when you may have more time to get involved in asking children what they plan to do, and in detailed discussions of outcomes; or at the end of an adult-led, small group activity, where the learning intention is clear and the session is short enough for children to remember!

How are we managing feedback so it does not become a pressure on us or on the children? Do we sometimes ask children what they are intending to do during child-initiated activities? Do we follow this up with conversations about how successful they are in reaching their own goals? Do we make our intentions clear for adult-led activities, so children know clearly when they have achieved them?

Examples of the process in action

One of the most useful ways to understand AfL in the early years is through examples of the process in action, in visits to settings where practitioners are trying the methods; by listening to or reading about practitioners as they talk or write about what they do; or by reading case studies and snippets of practice. Of course these can only give glimpses into the lives of children in our settings, but may help confirm what we know should be happening as we support children in thinking about learning.

Here are some examples:

Trisha is playing with Garry, a baby who is just learning to walk unaided. She holds his hands and says 'Let's try that again - that's right, move one foot at a time. Can you let go of my hand? Good balancing!'

Although Garry may not be able to understand everything Trisha is saying, he knows she is concentrating on him and she is clear about what she is giving praise for, not just saying 'Good boy'.

Neil brings his wobbly 'junk' model of a truck to show Sara, and as he reaches her two wheels fall off. Sara helps him to pick them up, saying, 'You said you were going to make a model today, and you have. It looks very interesting, tell me about it.' ''s a truck like my dad's' says Neil. 'Your dad sometimes lets you sit in his truck, doesn't he?' Neil nods. 'How did you make it?' 'Boxes and glue' says Neil. 'What happened to the wheels?' 'Falled off.' 'How could you fix them on better, so they don't fall of when you take it home?' 'More tape.' 'Let's go to the making table and see if we can find some, then maybe you'd like to take a photo?'

Sara confirms what Neil said his intentions were, gives plenty of praise, a suggestion that he could improve the truck, and a way of recording what he has done, so he can take his model home.

Four girls are playing in the outside area. They are making a den with some fabric and canes, but they are having problems making the den stay up so they can play inside. They see Colleen (a practitioner) and ask her to help. They want her to fix the den for them, but she has different ideas! 'Can you fix this den?' the girls ask. 'What are you trying to do? If you explain, I can help <u>you</u> to do it' says Colleen, 'What do you think you need?' The girls explain what they want to do.

'We need some clips to fix the material' says one girl. 'Do you know where to find them?' says Colleen. 'I do' says another girl. The two go off to search and soon come back with some pegs. 'We found some string too' they say. Building continues, with Colleen playing her part as a member of the group, leaving when the structure is stable and the girls can use it for their play. Later, she asks the

girls to tell her how the game went. The girls are enthusiastic about their den and their intentions to return to it tomorrow to make improvements and decorate the outside.

Colleen acts as a member of the group, modelling problem solving, not giving the answers. She does not solve their problems for them, asking open questions and gently pushing the solving of the problems back to the children. She stays with the group as they work on the structure, but leaves when she is no longer needed. She remembers to ask the girls to bring her up to date later and suggests they should tell the rest of the group how they made their den.

Two boys begin to shout and argue over the red bike in the pre-school. All the children think the red bike is the 'best bike', and there is always a rush to grab it at the beginning of the session. Nadia goes over to intervene, 'What is happening?' she says. 'I got it first!'. 'No, I got it first!' say the two boys, continuing to pull at the red bike. 'Please put the bike down while we talk about it' says Nadia, and the boys reluctantly let go.

'I know you both want the bike, what can we do about that?' says Nadia. Both children are still very upset and neither speaks. 'Well, what did we say yesterday when Jay and Jamie both wanted the bike?' 'Share it' says one. 'Yes, share it, and how did we agree to do that?' 'With the timer.' 'Yes, so do you want to get the timer and then we'll decide who is going first.'

The children go happily together and return with the sand timer. Nadia holds it behind her back (as agreed with the whole group) and the children guess which hand it is in. The boy who is right gets on the bike, while the other sits with Nadia, holding the timer. Nadia says to them 'You worked that out really well. What will you do next time you both want the bike?'

This situation is very common in early years settings where there is always the 'best bike' or an equivalent popular toy. The difference in this setting is that the practitioners helped the children to solve the problem and come up with a solution, which is now an expectation. Nadia knows that it takes time for children to get used to new arrangements. They are impetuous and need support to get things right. She praises them for remembering the new arrangement and reinforces what they should do next time.

Jamal is in his third term in Reception. He has been experimenting with mixing his own paint for a pattern-making activity. He brings his painting to show his teacher, Jan. She sits at a table and looks at the painting with Jamal.

'Well done', she says, 'you have made lots of colours by mixing the paints, how did you make the pattern?' Jamal smiles and points to the top of the paper 'I started the pattern here', he says, 'It's all squares and the colours go in turns.' 'I can see that', says Jan, tracing some of the squares with her finger, and saying the names of the colours. 'Was it a hard thing to do? How did you remember the pattern?' 'Yes, I kept forgetting the next colour!' says Jamal, 'but then I got it in my head and remembered it in my brain, it's brown, blue, red, green, brown, blue, red, green, and I kept saying it.' 'Good thinking, and good remembering.' Says Jan. 'I think we should take a photo and I'll write down how you remembered the pattern.' 'And put it in my red folder, and then I'm going to do another one – I know how to do it now, and this one will be much better!' says Jamal.

Careful, open questions, positively put, enable Jan to find out whether Jamal understands what the task was and whether he has achieved it. He is beginning to think about *how* he remembers things, and is feeling very successful. He is also able to set his own targets for improvement as he works on the second pattern.

The children in Acorn group are just embarking on a centre of interest about their local park, which they visit regularly throughout the year. They have just returned from an autumn walk with their pockets full of acorns and other things they have found. Lisa is working with them to think about what they have experienced and what they want to find out about. She sits with the children on the carpet, with a big piece of paper and some big felt-tipped pens, and reminds the children about what they were looking for today at the park. The children say 'autumn things', 'seeds', 'leaves', 'sticks'.

Lisa draws a picture of the park gates in the middle of the paper and begins to talk with the children about what they saw, heard, smelled, touched and even tasted at the park, framing their thoughts by using their senses. They start with things they saw. As they work on the mind map together, the children select from their collections and place them on the paper. Some children draw pictures of the things they saw or heard that they couldn't collect. Lisa prompts them to remember where they went and some of the things they heard or touched. They pass round the camera and look at the pictures they took, to remind themselves of what they chose to photograph.

Lisa also uses questions to encourage the children to think – 'What did we see at the other side of the pond?' 'Where did the dog go when he ran away? Who do you think he belongs to?' and 'Where is that thing you found Paul - that thing we didn't know the name of?' 'Can you remember what we wanted to find out about ducks?' 'We found some green tree seeds like wings, who brought those? How can we find out what they are?' 'What was that smell we smelled by the gate – the smell that made us all feel hungry?'

Lisa is skilfully scaffolding the children's learning as she takes them back through the walk in the park, reminding them of all the experiences they had, and helping them to shape them into some lines of enquiry for future learning, and further things to look for on their next visit. She will photograph the 3D mind map and use it as a centrepiece for a display that will grow during the next days and weeks as children find out more about autumn in their park. Their activities will involve painting, making collages and arrangements of the objects, bringing more findings to nursery, watching the weather, using simple reference books and telling stories about their own local park keeper who comes to visit and read *Percy the Park Keeper* with them.

I conclude this book here, firmly with the children, who are at the heart of the process of learning, supported by practitioners who are interested in them, not just as empty vessels to be filled and then measured, but as individuals, each one capable of thinking for themselves.

As the following quotes reinforce, children have a right to be in control of their own learning, we can't get inside their heads, but we can create a climate conducive to them doing it themselves!

'From the earliest age, the children should be involved and this is part of the assessment for learning process. The United Nations Convention on the Rights of the Child Article 12 states the right of the child to express an opinion and to have that opinion taken into account, in any matter or procedure affecting the child. Sharing the child's record together provides an ideal opportunity for celebrating achievements and discussing future plans. Even with babies it is a valuable chance to delight together in their achievements.'

Effective practice: Observation, Assessment and Planning
The Early Years Foundation Stage CD-ROM (DCSF, 2008)

'If we accept that learning is something that learners have to do (with our help), to improve the process of learning we must go beyond approaches that assume we can manage learning on pupils' behalf.

The more we can do to help them master the skills of learning, the more able they will be to manage it themselves. If they have to construct their own learning, it makes sense to help them to do it better!'

Assessment for Learning: A Practical Guide (CCEA, 2009)

Catching them at it!

Guy Claxton's *Building Learning Power* (2002) deals with the practical application of his ideas. In it he introduces us to four new 'Rs' that he would like to see replace the three traditional ones:

'Resilience: "being ready, willing and able to lock on to learning". Being able to stick with difficulty and cope with feelings such as fear and frustration.

Resourcefulness: "being ready, willing and able to learn in different ways". Having a variety of learning strategies and knowing when to use them.

Reflection: "being ready, willing and able to become more strategic about learning". Getting to know our own strengths and weaknesses.

Relationships: "being ready, willing and able to learn alone and with others".'

'"The flow experience acts as a magnet for learning"
                                                                    (Csikszentmihalyi, 2002)

Csikszentmihalyi's 'flow' metaphor describes how engaged we are in what we're doing. From the learner's perspective, the factors most likely to lead to flow are:

- clear learning intentions;
- feedback that helps us know how we're progressing;
- challenge that's sufficiently stretching;
- skills that are appropriate for the challenge; and
- lack of fear of failure.'

Assessment for Learning: A Practical Guide (CCEA, 2009)

Further reading

Are You Ready For Your Inspection? *A Guide to Inspections of Provision on Ofsted's Childcare and Early Years Registers*; OFSTED; 2009

Assessment and Reporting Arrangements 2010 (ARA); Qualifications and Curriculum Agency; 2009

Assessment and Reporting Arrangements 2011: Key Stage 1 (ARA); Qualifications and Curriculum Development Agency; 2010

Assessment for Learning*: A Practical Guide*; The Council for the Curriculum, Examinations and Assessment (Northern Ireland); 2009

Creating the Picture; Department for Education and Skills (England); 2007

Curriculum for Excellence, Building the Curriculum 5*: A Framework for Assessment*; The Scottish Government; 2010

'Early Years Education: An International Perspective'; Tony Bertram and Chris Pascal; Centre for Research in Early Childhood, Birmingham UK; 2002

Early Years Foundation Stage Profile Handbook; Qualifications and Curriculum Authority (England); 2008

Education (Pupil Information) (England) Regulations; 2005; www.legislation.gov.uk

Educating Young Children: Active Learning Processes for Preschool and Childcare Programs; Hohmann, Mary and Weikart, David P.; High/Scope Publications; 2002

Effective practice: Observation, Assessment and Planning; *The Early Years Foundation Stage* CD-ROM; Department for Children, Schools and Families (England); 2008

Engaging Parents and Children in EYFS Profile Assessment; National Assessment Agency (England); 2008

Excellence and Enjoyment*: Learning and Teaching in the Primary Years,* ***Planning and Assessment for Learning***; Professional development materials; Department for Children, Schools and Families (England); 2005

Foundation Phase Child Development Profile Guidance; Department for Children, Education, Lifelong Learning and Skills (Wales); 2009

Framework for Children's Learning for 3-7 Year Olds in Wales; Department for Children, Education and Lifelong Learning and Skills; 2008

Improving Outcomes for Children in the Foundation Stage *in Maintained Schools*; *Process-based Targets in the Foundation Stage*; Department for Children, Schools and Families (England); 2006

'Inside the Black Box: Raising Standards Through Classroom Assessment'; Paul Black and Dylan William; King's College London School of Education; 2001

Learning, Playing and Interacting: Good Practice in the Early Years Foundation Stage; Department for Children, Schools and Families (England); 2009

Observing Children; Department for Children, Education, Lifelong Learning and Skills (Wales); 2008

Seeing Steps in Children's learning – booklet and DVD; Qualifications and Curriculum Authority (England); 2005

Statutory Framework for the Early Years Foundation Stage; Department for Children, Schools and Families (England); 2008

Te Whariki, Early Childhood Curriculum; Ministry of Education (New Zealand); 1996

'The Nature and Value of Formative Assessment for Learning'; Paul Black; King's College London School of Education; 2004

Understanding the Foundation Stage; Early Years Inter-board publication: The Council for the Curriculum, Examinations and Assessment (Northern Ireland); 2006

Unlocking Formative Assessment, Practical Strategies for Enhancing Pupils' Learning in the Primary Classroom; Clarke, Shirley; Hodder Education; 2001